Opera People

Opera People

Photographs
Christian Steiner

Text
Robert M. Jacobson

Introduction
Michael Scott

THE VENDOME PRESS
NEW YORK PARIS

For John Coveney and Dario Soria

Edited by Alexis Gregory and Daniel Wheeler
Designed by Marlene Rothkin Vine and Peter Rauch

First Published in 1982 in Great Britain
by Weidenfeld & Nicolson Ltd., London
Copyright © 1982 The Vendome Press
Illustrations copyright © 1982 Christian Steiner
Published in the United States of America and Canada
by The Vendome Press, 515 Madison Avenue, New York, N.Y. 10022
Distributed in the United States of America
by The Viking Press, 40 West 23rd Street, New York, N.Y. 10010
Distributed in Canada by Methuen Publications

Library of Congress Cataloging in Publication Data
Steiner, Christian.
  Opera people.
    1. Singers—Portraits.   2. Conductors (Music)—
Portraits.   I. Jacobson, Robert M.   II. Title.
ML87.S8   779'.2'0924   82-7113
                        AACR2

ISBN 0-86565-038-1
Printed and bound in Italy

Contents

Introduction

The earliest opera that has survived all the way into this, the ninth, decade of the twentieth century is Peri's *Eurydice,* a work first heard in 1600, almost four hundred years ago. Throughout all those ages, until the outbreak of World War I, opera remained one of the most important entertainments of the civilized world. After 1918 the profoundest holocaust that man had hitherto known abruptly swept aside the old society and its agreeable pastimes. From the New World, where generations of Europeans had fled, came the American troops, bringing with them a taste for diversions more in tune with a democratic age. From America came the movies, which created their own idols—silent ones—to topple the diva from her traditional throne, as well as spectacles too vast to be contained on any opera house stage. The same nation also produced a new music, enchanting the post-war world with the heady tunes and foot-tapping rhythms of jazz. Opera seemed old-fashioned, and the opera house, with its frills and furs, serried tiers of boxes and dingy gallery, a metaphor for an outdated order, for a polite and elegant but rigidly stratified society.

Not that opera has lost its popularity. On the contrary, modern mechnization has vastly increased the performances of every kind of music. If numbers were all that mattered, then opera must be deemed far more popular today than ever it was in the past. Television transmitted simultaneously throughout the world—from Milan, Bayreuth, or Salzburg—assures, even in one broadcast, a far bigger audience than would have been possible at all the *stagione* performances lumped together since the beginning of opera's history. Yet, the fact remains, opera has ceased to be a vigorous art form as far as the creation of major new vehicles is concerned. The works of Mozart, Verdi, Wagner, and Puccini were famous in the composers' own lifetimes and have remained so ever since, but nothing produced in the last half-century has approached, never mind challenged, their popularity, or seems likely to do so. Many reasons account for this. Undoubtedly the growing complexity of modern society has something to do with it. The invention of the microphone, like the emergence of jazz and popular music, has ushered in a totally different kind of singer, one whose crooning (or yelling) can compete, effortlessly, with those possessed of naturally developed voices. Aided by modern technology, popular singers have access to audiences more numerous than could ever be accommodated at the largest theaters in the world. Indeed, the influence of electronic amplification has spread to the opera house, reinforcing the public taste for quantums of noise. It has also encouraged voices that sound big on records but are too throaty to

Christoph Willibald von Gluck

project clearly and effortlessly across a spacious auditiorium. On the radio, or phonograph records, it is unimportant whether a singer's voice projects or not, so long as it sounds effective. At best a record can only provide a two-dimensional account of a singer's art, even in stereophony, which is not a proper third dimension. Just listening to records will not give us much idea of the prodigious effect that a great voice—Nordica's, Destinn's, Flagstad's, or Nilsson's—created in the theater.

Two hundred and fifty years ago singers were opera's stars, before the conductor, stage director, and even the composer. If we look at the original Vienna cast of Gluck's *Orfeo*, in 1762, the name of the first Orfeo, the castrato Guadagni, lives on. So too does the composer, but the opera was not conducted like a modern performance, nor was it stage-directed. The director and the conductor became necessary at stagings long after the piece had been composed, their function being to reconcile the work to the taste of a modern audience. In the eighteenth century, Italian opera was sung in England or Germany by Italians, and in the Italian language, even if the composer was an Englishman or a German—Handel, for example. The vast majority of the audience knew no Italian. For them, what mattered was the singer's ability to create an effect with his voice—that is, convey the drama through the music. Composers such as Handel and Gluck understand this to perfection, for their music is written expressively, even eloquently, for the human voice.

And it did not happen accidentally. The greatest singers in history lived at this time—the castratos. They retained the pitch and quality of a boy's voice, albeit enhanced and developed by maturity, then powered by the lungs and diaphragm of a grown man. Mutilation may have been drastic, but the result—for music—was brilliant. It provided an irresistible combination, one that nature had deliberately avoided—the boy's naturally affecting cry delivered with the strength and surety of a man. Little wonder then that we find male sopranos referred to, by Pietro della Valle, as *soprani naturali*, in contrast to "artificial" sopranos, the falsettists. The practice of castration is as old as civilization, but, in the West at any rate, it was not until the sixteenth century that the operation was performed solely for musical reasons— in order to provide a substitute for women singers, who were banished by Pauline dictum from participation in church music. Enough of their music survives, complete with the original embellishments, to leave no doubt, according to Paul Henry Lang, that the *castrati* commanded an incomparable art not remotely approached in modern times. Their

Gioacchino Antonio Rossini

accomplishments were codified in various treatises, by Tosi and Mancini; moreover, they are implicit in the writings of Garcia, Faure, and Marchesi, and of virtually every voice pedagogue since. The remarkable musical talent of the *castrati* enabled them to improvise all manner of vocal figures and inform them with genuine musical feeling. As described by Dr. Burney, the prowess of Farinelli, probably the greatest singer in history, who became a minister in the government of Philip V of Spain, not only exceeded all his contemporaries, but in purity of tone, celerity of technique, dynamic control, flexibility, and exactitude of intonation, he established standards that remain unequaled. In England, Spain, Germany, and Austria, as well as in Italy, the initial popularity of opera owed much to the domination of the *soprani naturali*. They brought the art of singing to heights that have not been matched since. Altogether their reign lasted about two centuries, and the last of them, Giam Battista Velluti, sang in London in the 1820s.

In the days of Lully and Rameau, the native French singers put clarity of pronunciation first, with consequences that, inevitably, were musically compromising. France at that time boasted one of the most vigorous and brilliant of all theatrical traditions, and the declamatory style demanded by the tragedies of Corneille and Racine carried over into and influenced the lyric drama. Throughout the eighteenth century, as Dr. Burney, Baron Grimm, and other writers confirm, France provided no home for *bel canto*. French singing was provincial, lacking the virtuosity that made the Italians supreme. Before science mistook voice production for singing and while singers still learned their art by imitation, the French suffered for want of the best examples, the castratos. French audiences in the Age of Enlightenment found them unsightly, a reaction that did credit to their sensibilities but little good for their singers. It was not until after the Revolution, and the establishment of the Théâtre des Italiens in Paris in 1801, that a change came about. Paradoxically, at the very time when the castratos had lost their popularity in Italy, one of the last, Girolamo Crescentini, arrived in Paris and enjoyed a considerable success; even Napoleon was affected by his singing.

In the first quarter of the nineteenth century, the new Romantic style produced a significant development in the repertory of singers. This was caused by a gradual increase in the size and power of the orchestra, and with it the more emphatic accents required from the singer to give full expression to Romantic melodrama. To our ears, the Rossini orchestra sounds very small, but the composer's

Isabella Colbran

contemporaries thought quite otherwise. Indeed, Lord Mount-Edgcumbe was forever bewailing the din that the great Italian had unleashed, and Isabella Colbran, Madame Rossini in real life and a famous singer, lost her voice in a comparatively short time singing her husband's operas. In 1817, when Rossini wrote *Armida* for her, the range extended frequently to top C, but by *Semiramide*, in 1823, the score was much less heavily orchestrated, and the only high notes for the sporano, A's and B-flats, came in ensembles. The following year she retired. Colbran, like her succesors Giuditta Pasta and Maria Malibran, had a low voice. Her high notes, by general consensus, were the products of art rather than nature. Thus, they soon proved unequal to the demands made of them. Although suitable for ornamentation, they were not the characteristic part of the voice, a fact that allowed them neither the power nor the brilliance for declamation or bravura.

The second quarter of the century brought forth a higher and brighter type of voice, one which suited that quintessentially Romantic conceit, the fey and hapless heroine: Bellini's Amina and Elvira or Donizetti's Lucia. Unequivocally sopranos were Henrietta Sontag, Fanny Persiani, Angelina Bosio, and Jenny Lind. Before the end of the century theirs had become, in the persons of Adelina Patti, Christine Nilsson, Etelka Gerster, and Emma Albani, the prevailing type of *prima donna* voice. Meanwhile, the French taste introduced a dramatic soprano with a higher range than that of Colbran, Pasta, or Malibran, a performer capable of giving full expression to her voice in the works of the Grand Opéra. Among the most acclaimed were Rosine Stoltz and Cornélie Falcon, whose repertory reveals a simple, unflorid, and dramatic line leading to high C. Stoltz was the first Odette in Halévy's *Charles VI,* and she also created Zaïde in Donizetti's Grand Opéra *Don Sebastien.* Falcon lent her name to a whole repertory, only a few of which parts she actually sang, but these included Rachel in Halévy's *La Juive* and Valentine in Meyerbeer's *Les Huguenots.* In certain early editions of the latter score, Meyerbeer gives some guidance in casting since the largely concerted music written for Valentine makes transposition virtually impossible. He also helped establish the lyric soprano, a singer with neither the weight for dramatic parts nor the agility for "coloratura" roles. In Gounod's Marguerite she finally found her legitimacy.

The dramatic soprano, however, was not wholly a French prerogative. The Germans produced Wilhelmine Schröder-Devrient, who sang Agathe, Euryanthe, and the *Fidelio* Leonore. Eventually she became the first to attempt the Wagnerian roles of Adriano in *Rienzi,* Senta, and Venus. Although not wholly successful in this repertory, Schröder-Devrient blazed a trail that others could follow, notably Teresa Tietjens and Lilli Lehmann. Tietjens was a consummate vocalist, who sang with equal skill in the German repertory, from Mozart's Pamina to Wagner's Ortrud, and she also won praise for her Medea, Norma, Lucrezia Borgia, and Semiramide—so much so that Patti, notwithstanding the natural ascendancy of her voice, refrained from adding the last-named part to her repertory until after Tietjens' untimely death. Lehmann did not have such a remarkable voice, though she sang 128 roles, from the Queen of the Night to Brunnhilde, via Norma, Violetta, and Carmen.

The Italian dramatic soprano appeared much later than her counterparts in France and Germany, and she did not achieve complete definition until the arrival of the verismo repertory in the closing years of the nineteenth century. Meanwhile, parts like Verdi's Eboli and Amneris, Donizetti's Leonora in *La Favorita,* and Ponchielli's Laura in *La Gioconda* ushered in the mezzo-soprano, a new and higher type of voice than the contralto of Ernestine Schumann-Heink or Clara Butt. The virtual disappearance of the contralto voice is not, as has been suggested, the result of a mutation of nature, but rather of a change in taste and the predominance of a different operatic repertory.

Nor were female voices the only ones to be affected by the demands of the Romantic repertory. For a time the tenor maintained a level of accomplishment somewhat like that of his predecessor the castrato. It was not until the end of the first quarter of the nineteenth century, when sexual passion began to be represented in opera, that the tenor voice assumed characteristics which we would recognize. While Rossini was in Naples three remarkable tenors sang at the San Carlo: Andrea Nozzari, Giovanni David, and Manuel Garcia *père*. The roles he wrote for them were highly florid and prodigious in range, extending to top C, sometimes C-sharp, even D. But after his departure for Paris, Rossini simplified the ornamentation he wrote there to suit the French taste. Not untypically, two of the outstanding tenors in the succeeding generation were French: Adolphe Nourrit and Gilbert-Louis Duprez. Duprez made history by becoming the first to take high C from the chest. The effect was stunning, and its influence is still felt today. Even more spectacular, however, was the singing of an Italian, Giovanni Battista Rubini. The tale of his accidentally misreading high F for D-flat, during a rehearsal of

Giovanni Battista Rubini

Arturo Toscanini

Puritani, and of Bellini's decision to mark the note in the score, much to the embarrassment of every Arturo since, has become legend. The F, of course, would have been in falsetto. The low male voices too felt the urge to produce brilliant and strenuous high notes. In the days of Handel, and even of Mozart, the baritone as such did not exist, although many leading roles that the 18th-century loosely designated first-bass parts—Figaro or Don Giovanni, for example—are today described as baritones. The Figaro of *Il Barbiere di Siviglia* is generally considered the first unequivocally baritone role. Despite some maverick high notes in the latter's "Largo al factotum" (for which, it has been conjectured, Rossini had special reasons), it was not until the time of Verdi, whose partiality for the upper fifth of the vocal range is nowhere more apparent than in his baritone roles, that the high-low male voice developed its own characteristics.

In the wake of Rossini came Donizetti, Bellini, and Meyerbeer, whose works were sung in the next half-century by Fodor-Mainvielle, Cinti Damoreau, Nourrit, Dorus-Gras, Duprez, Falcon, Stoltz, Roger, and Faure, all as distinguished as their Italian contemporaries. Throughout this priod France remained the dominant power on the Continent. It had, after all, taken the entire force of the Allies to defeat Napoleon. Paris constituted a mecca to which even the likes of Verdi and Wagner, who professed to disdain France and its culture, felt themselves obliged to journey. But after the humiliating defeat of the Franco-Prussian War (1870) and the bloody events of the ensuing Commune, Paris lost much of its international prestige and along with this its overriding importance as a cultural center. With Germany in the ascendant and the unification of Italy completed, Wagner and Verdi were content to succeed first at home and then wait for Paris to capitulate.

The late nineteenth century saw the advent of the star conductor, whose effect has proved quite as telling as that of the singer. One of the first was Arturo Toscanini. As far back as the second quarter of the nineteenth century Rossini and Donizetti had been involved in the musical direction of their own operas. Then, later on, Verdi too had conducted many of his operas, but not after *Don Carlo.* By the turn of the century the gradual revival of earlier music made it inevitable that the conductor would assume the role of the first musical authority. By Toscanini's time—when many composers (like Puccini) were incapable of conducting or (like Verdi) had died, and music, through the rapid growth of Western populations and the emerging importance of the phonograph, had become much more diverse—it was logical to accept the conductor as the medium through which the composer's intentions should be expressed. Nowadays Toscanini's reputation rests, to a large extent, on the recordings the maestro made in the last part of his life. They preserve something of his extraordinary energy, though too often this degenerates into a frenzy. His tyrannical manner in rehearsals cowed the players, and it would be interesting to know whether it was his reputation or his technique that creates the recorded results. The former would seem more likely. A performance of the fourth act from *Rigoletto* (with Milanov, Merriman, Peerce, and Warren) recorded in 1944 is like a ghostly parody—the emphasis falling on the orchestral playing rather than on the singing. No doubt the orchestra does play remarkably, but Verdi, it ought not to be forgotten, wrote *Rigoletto* for the singers first. Fossilization seems to have been inevitable once opera was no longer led by its composers but by conductors.

Some confirmation of this process may be had if we compare the repertory of operas mounted at New York's Metropolitan Opera in 1883, the company's first season, with those presented at roughly twenty-five-year intervals throughout the twentieth century. In 1883 the bulk of the repertory was still contemporary, for even the oldest work, *Don Giovanni*, had yet to reach its centenary. Chronologically the selection continued with *Barbiere, Sonnambula,* and *Roberto il Diavolo,* then upwards of fifty years old. The rest included *Puritani, Lucia di Lammermoor; Les Huguenots, Marta, Le Prophète, Lohengrin, Rigoletto, Trovatore, Traviata, Faust,* and five pieces still less than two decades on the stage: *Mignon, Amleto, Mefistofele, Carmen,* and *Gioconda.* A quarter of a century later, in the 1908 season (the first that Toscanini conducted), the repertory ranged back to *Le Nozze di Figaro* (then 122 years old), *Fidelio* (133), and *Barbiere* (just over 90). Later works included Donizetti's *L'Elisir d'Amore, Lucia,* and *Don Pasquale,* all of them familiar for more than six decades. Five of the season's operas had been composed between 1845 and 1859: *Tannhäuser, Rigoletto, Trovatore, Traviata,* and *Faust.* The 1860s and '70s had produced Smetana's *Die Verkaufte Braut,* Verdi's *Aida,* and Wagner's *Ring.* Two scores had had their first hearing in 1884: Massenet's *Manon* and Puccini's *Le Villi.* More than 10 but less than 20 years old were *Cavalleria Rusticana* and *I Pagliacci,* Catalani's *La Wally,* Verdi's *Falstaff,* and Puccini's *La Bohème.* Finally, the Met's 1908 audience saw three new operas: *Tosca,* which had premiered in 1900; *Madama Butterfly,* dating from 1906; and d'Albert's *Tiefland,* then scarcely a year old. Altogether, a perfectly balanced repertory.

In 1933 the Met again presented three new operas: Deems Taylor's *Peter Ibbetson*, Howard Hanson's *Merry Mount,* and Louis Gruenberg's *The Emperor Jones*, all premiered at the house but the last two known from previous seasons. None, as it turned out, could match the success even of d'Albert's *Tiefland,* never mind *Tosca* or *Butterfly.* The oldest opera in the repertory was once more *Don Giovanni,* now nearly a century and a half old, followed by *Lucia* and *Linda di Chamounix,* both of them dating back more than 90 years. The next oldest works were *Tannhäuser* and *Lohengrin* and, from Verdi's middle period, *Rigoletto, Trovatore,* and *Traviata,* succeeded by a group of various pieces: Gounod's *Faust,* Wagner's *Tristan und Isolde,* Meyerbeer's *L'Africana,* Thomas's *Mignon,* and Gounod's *Roméo et Juliette.* The rest, save for *Salome* and *Gianni Schicchi,* had been written in the nineteenth century: *Aida,* the *Ring* cycle, *Simon Boccanegra, Lakmé, Mignon, Cavalleria, Pagliacci,* and *Hänsel und Gretel.*

By 1958 the fossilization of the Met's repertory is clearly apparent. *Don Giovanni* continued to be the oldest work mounted, its age rivaled only by that of *Die Zauberflöte.* But almost a half-century separated the Mozart operas from the next oldest score presented that year: *Lucia.* Then the historical succession unfolded with *Lohengrin, Rigoletto, Traviata,* and *Ballo in Maschera,* continuing with *Forza del Destino, Macbeth, Meistersinger,* and *Don Carlo,* all composed between 1847 and 1868. The 1870s had yielded Strauss's *Fledermaus,* Verdi's *Aida,* Moussorgsky's *Boris Godounov,* Bizet's *Carmen,* Ponchielli's *Gioconda,* Offenbach's *Les Contes d'Hoffmann,* and Tschaikovsky's *Eugene Onegin.* From the last two decades of the century the Met had Verdi's *Otello, Cav* and *Pag,* and Puccini's *Bohème* and *Tosca.* The only operas less than fifty years old were Berg's *Wozzeck* and Barber's *Vanessa,* a work actually commissioned by the Metropolitan and premiered there in 1958?

And in the 1982–83 season the Met seems to have changed its repertory hardly at all. *Idomeneo* replaces *Don Giovanni* as the oldest work, but *Bariere* and *Lucia* are still there (in fact, *Lucia* has made it at every quarter all the way back to 1883, in that year and in 1908 as a vehicle for Marcella Sembrich, in 1933 for Lily Pons, in 1958 for Roberta Peters, and now for Joan Sutherland). Then come *Tannhäuser, Trovatore, Ballo in Maschera, Forza del Destino, Macbeth, Don Carlo, Boris Godounov, Gioconda, Walküre, Les Contes d'Hoffmann, Parsifal, Hänsel und · Gretel, Bohème, Adriana Lecouvreur, Pelléas et Mélisande, Madama Butterfly, Rosenkavalier, L'Enfant et les Sortilèges,* and *Arabella.* Only Poulenc's *Les Mamelles de Tirésias,* first performed more than 35 years ago, in 1947, could be remotely described as modern.

Giacomo Puccini

Giuseppe Verdi

The first thing worth noting about this repertory is that almost all the works produced during the last hundred or so years are still known today. Even Thomas's *Hamlet* has recently been staged in Australia with Sherrill Milnes, who is to perform it in New York as well. Meyerbeer's *Roberto il Diavolo* had a revival at Florence in 1968 with Boris Christoff, while the Metropolitan mounted Flotow's *Martha* in 1961, with Victoria de los Angeles and Richard Tucker. The repertory up to 1908—except possibly for Puccini's *Le Villi* (which deserves a revival) and d'Albert's *Tiefland* (once a great favorite in Germany)—remains very familiar. By 1933, however, the management felt obliged to produce some new works. But the road to Hell is paved with operatic scores from the pens of eminently respectable composers. Scarcely a note from any one of the Met's novelties would be recognizable today. Only *The Emperor Jones* seems to have had anything like a recent revival, when in 1982 Serafin (the conductor at the original Met premier) led it in Italy with Rossi-Lemeni singing the title role.

The phonograph, which permits us to hear voices from the distant past, started to preserve contemporary performances at the precise moment that opera was being overtaken by the modern world. Was its invention simply a coincidence, or did it, albeit inadvertently, accelerate the decline of opera as a vital art form? Eighty years after the first phonograph records were made, the question remains. Undoubtedly the most famous singer of all those first recorded—his records now altered, adapted, and generally tampered with—was the tenor Caruso. There is good reason to ascribe the modern qualities in his voice to the phonograph, since Caruso was copied not just by singers who lived in his own day, but also by countless others who acknowledged him as master for more than three-quarters of a century. One could well wonder whether Caruso invented the phonograph or it invented him. Certainly the fact that his singing seems so modern could be the consequence of a taste that he was the first to anticipate. At the outset, his reputation was ambiguous, partly because of vocal problems, partly because the critics, accustomed to the old school, found it difficult to accept the newcomer's vehement and, frankly, more vulgar style. By 1902, however, when he made his first records for the Gramophone and Typewriting Company, the operas of the *versimo* were triumphant. Two years earlier, in performances of *La Bohème* at La Scala, after the critics and the box-holders had withheld their approbation, Caruso went over their heads and appealed to the gallery. It was a new century, and with it came the age of the common man. From that time dates the beginning of Caruso's greatness.

It is hardly surprising that the preoccupations of the world at large should have been mirrored in an art form as social as opera. At no time was the relationship between opera and society more evident than in the second half of the nineteenth century, when the most pressing issues of European politics, such as the various struggles for national independence, made themselves felt in a whole gamut of different operatic—hence vocal—styles, especially in France, Germany, and Russia. Until Mozart's time, the hegemony of the Italian style was complete, except in France, where, as Dr. Burney once again tells us, the singers were something of a bad joke. By 1900 the Italian style still had a few practitioners, though it was in eclipse, compromised by almost every composer and all the various national styles—eventually even by Italy's own verismo school. This does not mean that the music then being composed for the voice was wholly unvocal. In fact, virtually none of it was unvocal, a quality whose development would be left to the twentieth century. Yet much of the new music failed to be vocal in conception, since its awkward tessitura strangled the voice and made it impossible for the words to be easily pronounced. Nor was it solely in musical matters that the various national styles obtruded into the vocal art, which languages themselves modified. Singing had to assimilate such problematic sounds as the French nasal tone, the German hard consonants, and the Spanish aspirate. By the later nineteenth century, the classical style, where it survived, as in the art of Adelina Patti, came to be called *bel canto,* a term invented to distinguish it from much that was being passed off at the time as "beautiful singing." By the time of the phonograph, there were relatively few singers left "capable," in Hanslick's words, "of offering an utterly individual pleasure almost independent of the composition at hand."

Caruso was not the only remarkable singer active in the first years of the century. With the appearance of Feodor Chaliapin opera received one of its most potent and influential performers. The achievement of the great Russian bass must, in one respect, be considered greater than Caruso's. Thanks to the naturally affecting quality of higher voices, the tenor had been in the ascendancy since the days of Rubini, all the while that even the most renowned basses—Galli, Lablache, Edouard de Reszke, and Plançon—were being progressively reduced to subordinate roles. Now Chaliapin changed all that, not by trying to outmatch tenors in the production of top notes from the chest, or in passages of fioritura, but by moving stage center and becoming a principal player. No company could have afforded to waste him on *comprimario* roles, for he was the first bass ever to receive

Enrico Caruso

Feodor Chaliapin

a fee as high as that normally paid to the *primo tenore* or *prima donna*. Russian opera, until his time something provincial and obscure, gave Chaliapin the opportunity to achieve full expression for his histrionic and vocal genius, especially in the title role of Moussorgsky's *Boris Godounov,* which he popularized first in Russia, then throughout the rest of the world. Stamping his personality on the part, Chaliapin created a performing tradition that remains vital today. But he also transformed and expanded established conceptions of certain non-Russian roles, particularly Mephistopheles in the operas of Boito and Gounod.

The phonograph does not have the capability to preserve a singer's physical presence, yet Chaliapin's art was so integrated, his singing so completely identifiable that his records almost achieve the impossible. We can well believe that his histrionics were tremendous, for in the long phrases of Boris's farewell scene, he creates an effect quite as expressive solely through his singing. The voice is characteristic, the tone perfectly poised and limpid, the registers smoothly blended, and the mastery of the head voice complete. For him speech and song were indivisible; at its most intense speech simply turns into song and there is no mechanical adjustment. We can hear Chaliapin at his best in some live recordings made at Covent Garden, when he was in his midfifties and had been singing for more than thirty years. The extraordinary range of dynamics, through every nuance from a resonant forte to a hushed, yet always comfortably audible, pianissimo, was achieved entirely through intensity. Never was his singing loud or soft merely for its own sake, and however beautiful, every effect had its cause. By scorning the empty virtuosity that takes no account of words, he echoed the complaint made by Tosi two centuries earlier that singing which is instrumental in conception neglects the proper affections and disregards precisely that which makes the human voice unique: its ability to put words into the musical tone. In everything Chaliapin did there was an extraordinary spontaneity and intensity, both highly prized features of bel canto.

In the first years of this century, when the idiom of contemporary popular music still did not differ radically from operatic music, it was possible for a classically trained singer to have, as it were, a foot in both camps. Caruso enjoyed as much fame as a singer of Neapolitan songs and popular ballads as he did for his work at the opera house. Despite the increased size and power of the orchestra and the more dramatic manner of the newer music, the style remained a vocal one, and in this respect it was not radically dissimilar from

Beniamino Gigli

"nonclassical" music of the day. After World War I, however, the musical idioms began to grow rapidly apart. In the 1920's the shattering impact of jazz and the invention of the microphone led, as we have seen, to a dramatic development in popular music, which the phonograph carried to all corners of the civilized world. Meanwhile, modern opera was becoming more abstruse and modern classical music more incomprehensible to the layman. The popular songs that Gigli sang on the radio, on records, or in recital encouraged him to adopt a vulgarity of style throughout his art, provoking the critics' ire once he began tainting his operatic performances with the mannerisms that had proved so successful in the popular arena. These, however, were nothing more than an extension of the language of verismo, thus could conceivably be justified in the name of realism. And had opera developed along similar lines, there would have been no conflict. But the twenties coincided with the end of verismo and the drying up of that well of instantly seductive melody that for so long had sustained the appeal of opera. After the death of Puccini, save for a gesture or two by Zandonai and Pizzetti, it was exhausted. While popular music under fresh influences gained a new dynamism, opera settled for a period of revivals and retrospection.

During his years at the Metropolitan, Gigli sang in twenty-five operas, only five of which were modern compositions, and in rather more than half of the rest, his style, for all the beauty of the voice, clashed with the composer's. The complaining critics took it as their solemn duty to educate Gigli's taste, thereby reflecting the teutonic notion of high seriousness in Art. For them the opera house was a temple of enlightenment, not a theater of entertainment. Gigli's shameless courting of the gallery, "like a picturesque beggar suing for alms," as Newman put it, seemed little short of blasphemy. But the singer remained unrepentant, like all popular musicians, for as an entertainer he felt it necessary to keep in tune with the taste of the general public. What the critics said was beside the point. Apart from questions of money, Gigli would keep his appeal vigorous and fresh by broadening the base of his concert activities and by spending less time in opera. Despite the rapidly expanding popularity of motion pictures and jazz music, the Metropolitan's position continued unassailable—until the Crash of 1929. Now, the Great Depression revealed just how precarious were the theater's finances, since, for all classes of patrons, opera was—inevitably—one of the first places to economize. Faced with bankruptcy, the Met's management had no choice but to make stringent cuts in expenditure. And as might be expected, it turned to the artists who had enjoyed the fruits of prosperity and ought now, so the directors reasoned, to shoulder a share of the deficit. Many of them accepted the inevitable; they were hardly in a position to do otherwise, given the fact that opera companies elsewhere in the United States would take their cue from the Metropolitan.

In Europe, World War I took more than thirty years to resolve. During that time opera went on oblivious to the changing circumstances. Except in the German-speaking countries, the art of singing degenerated sharply. Italian opera became a prestigious aspect of the fascist government of Mussolini, and after Puccini, only a stream of nonentities came forward with new works. France, since 1870, had been in decline, but it took the best part of half a century for the nation to reach political torpor. The lowest ebb came in the years between the two World Wars, a time when Paris Opéra and the Opéra-Comique represented the nadir of taste. French singers were once again (as they had been before Rossini came to Paris) preoccupied with their language. Gounod and Massenet, for instance, had written *Faust* and *Werther,* both of which did well in translation, but *Pelléas et Mélisande* is unthinkable in any language other than French. In Britain the economic climate of the 1920's made any operatic activity virtually impossible. Only in Germany and Austria did singing improve, with the artists like Lehmann, Rethberg, Jeritza, Schumann, Tauber, Schwarz, and Kipnis. But with the shock of Nazi domination and the perversion of German culture, many of these singers went abroad, to Britain and the United States. Meanwhile, in Russia, except for an occasional reappearance by a prerevolutionary star, Nezhdanova or Sobinov for example, the singers might as well have not existed, so completely had an iron curtain descended.

By the end of World War II the prestige of opera had fallen far and the virtual curtailment of public funding had shrunk operatic activity to a bare minimum. It was not until the 1950's that economic revival made opera possible again, by which time the main impetus came from the stage director. In the prewar period, especially in Germany and Austria, there had been a large number of theatrical productions with all kinds of weird and wonderful scenery for plays or operas. Many stage directors, Carl Ebert for example, had worked in the opera houses of between-the-wars Germany. Max Reinhardt, as long ago as the end of World War I, had built an entire production of Offenbach's *Die schöne Helene* around the youthful beauty of Maria Jeritza. Many years later, the appearance of another soprano would once again revive opera. Who can deny that there are still singers, occasionally, more remarkable than any conductor or stage director?

Italy in the early 1950's saw the emergence of a soprano whose voice matched the quality of her remarkable talent. An elemental nature and the circumstances of life (and of the war) had kept her unaffected and relatively shielded from the world, with the result that her art had a force and a primal impact unlike anything seen or heard for several generations. (Was it only a coincidence that she was born exactly fifty years after her two great predecessors: Enrico Caruso and Feodor Chaliapin?) Maria Callas's life is worth recording. She was born in New York into a family of Greek immigrants and spent her early years in America, by all accounts not a conspicuously happy part of her life, before moving to Athens in the late 1930's. At that time Greece was a very poor and backward country, cut off from the rest of Europe. When the war came, bringing invasion and occupation to Greece, Callas had begun to sing with the Athens Opera. Of how she sang, unfortunately, we have no recorded evidence, although she did appear in a variety of roles. Among them, interestingly, was Beethoven's *Fidelio* (whether in German or Greek is not clear). After the war, in 1946, she made a futile trip to the United States. (We can only wonder what might have happened to her had she, and not Regina Resnik, accepted an invitation from the Metropolitan to sing Madame Butterfly in English.) What did transpire was that the tenor Giovanni Zenatello, then an agent, heard her, and offered the role of Gioconda at the Verona arena for the summer of 1947. The twenty-four-year-old Callas accepted, and then spent the following two years in Italy, getting married and undertaking a variety of dramatic roles, among them Turandot, Isolde, Kundry, Aida and Brunnhilde. While she was singing in *Die Walküre* (like her other Wagnerian parts, in Italian) at Venice in 1949, Serafin proposed that she accept to do Elvira in *I Puritani*, always considered a coloratura role. She did and created a sensation. From that moment on Callas was a *prima donna*. Within three years she had reached La Scala, where for her debut she sang Elena in Verdi's *Vespri Siciliani*. Then followed Norma, Leonora in *Trovatore*, Fiorilla in Rossini's *Turco in Italia*, Violetta, and Elvira in *Puritani*. Not since Lilli Lehmann had a soprano ventured such a wide-ranging repertory.

For the first time since the Toscanini era at the beginning of the century La Scala emerged as the world's leading opera house. In 1954 it attracted Luchino Visconti, one of Italy's foremost film and stage directors, who came and created a notable series of productions that expanded Callas's repertory to include *Vestale, Sonnambula, Traviata, Ifigenia in Tauride,* and *Anna Bolena.* With Franco Zeffirelli, a pupil of Visconti, she also did *Turco in Italia.* By her extraordinary musical

Lotte Lehmann

powers, Callas became a major influence, upsetting a century and a half of worn-out conventions. When she sang *Lucia,* the opera ceased to be the moribund failure that had had only a single performance at Covent Garden since the days of Tetrazzini, or at the Metropolitan where its decline could be measured by the fall in singing standards from Galli-Curci via Pons to Peters, until coloratura was only something for the birds. To understand the profound effect that Callas had on opera, we have only to compare her repertory with what had been presented some thirty years earlier. She may not have been the first to rediscover certain works; *Anna Bolena,* for example, had received a Scala production somewhat earlier. Still, it was Callas who, in fact, *revived* the piece. Her career at La Scala lasted a mere eleven years, scarcely a notable length of time by any standards. In her wake came Cerquetti and Souliotis, perhaps too much influenced by her to sing on their own for very long; Caballé, who has been able to succeed her as well as Grisi succeeded Pasta; and Sutherland, whose astonishing agility would not have been possible without Callas having re-established criteria of musical accuracy in florid singing. Afterwards appeared a whole raft of singers who may never have heard her but who were unwittingly influenced by the repertory that she had made popular, not only by her penetrating personality but also by her prodigious technical command. The shadow she casts over opera and singing gets longer with each passing year.

While the canon of operatic literature has remained the same and opera house repertories are virtually what they were half a century and more ago, modern technology—records and television—has rapidly made the operatic world a smaller place. Now we live in the age of the stage director. It has become Zeffirelli's *Otello,* not Solti's or Domingo's, and certainly not Verdi's! The composer, or his estate, does not even earn anything out of it anymore. Today singers are made rather than developed. Thirty years ago Joan Sutherland was Aida, Antonia in *The Tales of Hoffmann,* and Pamina in *The Magic Flute,* long before anyone would have had the wit—save for her husband—to invite her to sing Lucia. But all that has changed. A new young Italian soprano, Cecilia Gasdia, was discovered at a singing competition; already she has sung Luisa Miller, Giulietta in Bellini's *I Capuletti e i Montecchi,* and Anna Bolena. Nowadays television can reach the entire world in one broadcast, so that Agnes Baltsa, a Greek mezzo-soprano, was heard by many people for the first time singing Cenerentola's Rondo Finale in a gala concert with Domingo, Cappuccilli, and other established artists. Katia Ricciarelli was a name almost from the minute she started to sing. No doubt the publicity generated by such exposure will have no harmful effect on some singers; yet it would be hard to imagine what contribution it could have made to Caruso, who spent more than a half a decade refining his technique in small Italian opera houses, or to Chaliapin, who was way ahead of New York when he first sang there in 1908, or to Callas, who had to fight all kinds of hostility, real or imagined, until she became famous.

In many ways this book is part and parcel of modern publicity. Christian Steiner—one of the world's leading photographers of singers and artists—works constantly on commission to do pictures for personal publicity and promotion, for record covers and concert tours. As artists fly in and out, he catches them on the wing, superstars glittering in the spotlights whose very human aspect he captures on film. Endless stories in the press, bestselling books, and television interviewers have generated enormous interest in opera people, for it is probably thanks to them, the most dynamic element in opera, that the medium continues to thrive, albeit the captive of its past, in an age when all other art forms have undergone enormous change.

Michael Scott

The
Singers

Joan Sutherland

A natural phenomenon, somewhere in the league with Niagara Falls, the Grand Canyon, the Amazon River, or the Alps, is the only way to characterize Joan Sutherland. Bigger than life, awesome in so many ways, and, yes, natural, she is at the same time a miraculous product of grueling study and preparation. Sutherland, more than anyone else, has made the singing world aware of just how brilliant pyrotechnics can be—trills, roulades, arpeggios, *fioriture* of every imaginable kind, all executed with the most exalted refinement. Probably no one can ever forget hearing Joan Sutherland for the very first time, since the sheer size and weight of her sound combine with a spectacular upper extension, all the way to rock-solid E-naturals above high C, to make the soprano unique in the annals of modern operatic singing.

The fluency, the high notes, the bel canto style, the technical virtuousity came through the vision of her husband, the conductor-pianist Richard Bonynge, a fellow Australian who began to develop Sutherland's vocal facility and style during her early days at London's Covent Garden in the mid-1950s. At that time the singer, who had won several prizes in her native country and had come to England for further study, was performing small roles—Clothilde to Maria Callas's Norma, for instance—and preparing such parts as Amelia in *Un Ballo in Maschera,* Agathe in *Der Freischütz,* and others, convinced that she was a spinto or dramatic soprano. Although one of her audition pieces was Elvira's "Qui la voce" from *I Puritani,* the very amplitude of the voice, matched with a large-scale 5'8" physique, made it seem as if Sutherland were destined for a Wagnerian future. Meanwhile, she found success as Olympia in *Les Contes d'Hoffmann* and as Gilda in *Rigoletto,* which confirmed once and for all that Bonynge's view of her talents was absolutely on target.

Then came 1959, the breakthrough year, when Covent Garden made Sutherland the centerpiece of a new production of Donizetti's *Lucia di Lammermoor,* directed by Franco Zeffirelli and conducted by Tullio Serafin, the venerable maestro who had done so much to develop the talents of Rosa Ponselle and Maria Callas, among others. While the public cheered, critics grasped for adjectives to describe the debutant's stunning agility and ringing tone, her full-throated, theater-filling outbursts, plus the dazzling ease above high C, the clear articulation, the runs, the brilliant attacks, and every other item in the battery of bel canto fireworks. Sutherland truly affected the role of the mad Scottish lassie, chasing her own coruscating tones from one side of the stage to the other. The audience sat hypnotized until the end of the climactic scene—then erupted into thunderous approval. And the timing proved just right, for by now Maria Callas was lost to us as lunatic Lucy. Suddenly the world of opera had entered the Sutherland era. And if the new wonder's personality did not haunt quite as the Callas one had, Sutherland compensated with other, more purely vocal qualities, making those standard, birdlike varieties of Lucia seem pale indeed. *La Divina* had given way to *La Stupenda,* as the great Australian came to be known in European circles.

A true dramatic coloratura, Sutherland is a throwback to the singers of another century. And London/Decca Records immortalized that image early on in a two-record set entitled *The Art of the Prima Donna,* where Sutherland—quite rightly—aligned herself with the legendary coloratura sopranos from the eighteenth century onward: Catalini, Malibran, Lind, Patti, Melba, Galli-Curci. The connection was proper in other respects as well, since her mother and first teacher had possessed an important mezzo voice and had studied with a pupil of Mathilde Marchesi, the famed teacher of Melba, Eames, and Calvé. With the plums of the bel canto repertory in hand, Sutherland immediately entered the arena of Europe's leading theaters, there undertaking Beatrice di Tenda, Marguerite in *Les Huguenots,* Elvira in *I Puritani,* Handel's Alcina, Rossini's *Semiramide,* and Amina in *La Sonnambula.* Eventually came Bellini's Norma, which the singer first essayed in 1965 at Vancouver, having waited until she felt ready for this summit of the repertory. Both Sutherland and Bonynge view the part in the light of its having been sung by Pasta, the first Amina, and their approach remained true to bel canto ideals, without the patina of verismo that many other singers have brought to the role of the Druid priestess.

Sutherland came to the Metropolitan Opera in 1961–62, her international reputation already firmly established and the New York public prepared to acclaim a new star. Vancouver had already seen her North American debut a few years earlier,

thanks to the bass-baritone George London, who had heard her in Europe and extolled her virtues wherever he went. New York ultimately did not get as much of Sutherland as she was willing to give. Rudolf Bing, seeming to resist the tide of the bel canto revival, stingily doled out precious few crumbs: *La Sonnambula, Norma, La Fille du Régiment,* and a new *Lucia.* Otherwise, the soprano comfortably fitted into revivals of *La Traviata, Don Giovanni, Rigoletto.* Almost as divine revenge, in the immediate wake of Bing's retirement, she stood as the crown jewel in one of the handsomest, most stirring, and perfect bel canto revivals of our day: the 1975–76 Sandro Sequi staging of *I Puritani* with Luciano Pavarotti. It is impossible to erase the image of her descending Ming Cho Lee's broad, steep stairs in Act II as she plaintively uttered "Qui la voce." This was the early Romantic spirit in its true reincarnation, and it came and went in one season, like some kind of rare, mysterious bird. Those "loony dames," as the diva calls them, have long been her strongest suit. The next season she returned to New York with true exotica, Massenet's *Esclarmonde,* which she had previously revivified in San Francisco. Elsewhere, around the globe, audiences have observed her Merry Widow, Lucrezia Borgia, Maria Stuarda, Lakmé, Rosalinda—the list runs on and on. Luciano Pavarotti says he learned how to breathe and support his voice from singing with her. Together Sutherland and Bonynge have taught a whole generation of opera lovers something about the art of nineteenth-century singing. We may criticize her diction, her lack of dramatic flair, or any number of small points, but the fact remains that Joan Sutherland—now Dame Joan—towers as a natural phenomenon.

Joan Sutherland and Richard Bonynge

Elisabeth Schwarzkopf

Stunning and unforgettable, Elisabeth Schwarzkopf reigned supreme in the jewels of Mozart and Strauss. In the concert hall she became the Hugo Wolf stylist *in excelsis*. While early in her career, particularly in London during the postwar years, her repertory claimed such staples as Mimi in *La Bohème*, Violetta in *La Traviata*, and Madama Butterfly, she came to be closely identified with the Countess of *Le Nozze di Figaro*, Donna Elvira of *Don Giovanni*, Fiordiligi of *Così fan Tutte*, as well as perhaps her most celebrated role, the Marschallin of *Der Rosenkavalier*. She took these roles, as well as the Countess in *Capriccio*, and made them her own, everywhere opera was performed, always leaving behind an indelible impression. In Schwarzkopf one felt the timeless Viennese tradition, for she combined a pungent style with breathtaking physical allure, a sense of the distant, the unobtainable.

Schwarzkopf's entry into America wasn't an easy one. In the early 1950s the ravages of World War II were still being felt, strongly. Town Hall, the scene of her first American recital in 1953, had to be heavily guarded, for no one knew what kind of protest would greet this superb artist of German background who had spent the war years singing in Central Europe. But she came and she conquered, her formidable aristry, honed to perfection, overcoming any political questions. Her recitals soon became nectar for the connoisseur, climaxed by a magnificent farewell to America during the 1974–75 season at New York's Carnegie Hall. One made pilgrimages to Schwarzkopf evenings to receive the final word not only on Wolf but also on Schubert, Brahms, Schumann, Strauss, the classics of the German lied. As she said some years back, a singer must have historical awareness of the style involved and be aware of the connotations that are part of any language. "Much as I've tried to sing in French and other languages, I do not think that it is possible to sing lieder and songs in other than your native tongue. You have to grow up in the language to know the meanings behind the words, so that all the related images that create the colors of what you sing can spring to your mind. The ambiance of a word is what is so crucial. Take the word *Wald* for instance—it has different connotations in a poem by Mörike or Eichendorff or Goethe, or in a setting by Schubert or Wolf or Brahms. Each word is different for every composer, poet, and poem....and you cannot possibly begin to learn these things. They are what you grow up with and absorb unconsciously."

Besides her own immersion in this music, Schwarzkopf was lucky to have been married to the distinguished record producer Walter Legge, who brilliantly carved her career both on records and on the stage. He believed a great singer had an easily recognizable, unforgettable personal timbre, and together they played records of Rosa Ponselle, Meta Seinemeyer, Lotte Lehmann, Elisabeth Schumann, Frida Leider, and others—as well as such instrumentalists as Fritz Kreisler and Artur Schnabel—and in due course Schwarzkopf developed her own distinctive qualities. The couple worked tirelessly on refining her art, going over songs time and again, often driving her accompanist to distraction. Nuance, subtlety, emotional detail, everything was examined under a microscope with a kind of mania for perfection, and Schwarzkopf's performances represented the culmination of such painstaking care.

Earlier, she had studied with the legendary coloratura soprano Maria Ivogün, who encouraged her to go on the recital stage. At that time, Schwarzkopf possessed a high, easy voice for Zerbinetta, Rosina, Constanze, Oscar, and Musetta. After the war there emerged a close-knit Viennese ensemble with Jurinac, Welitsch, Seefried, Streich, and others in the works of Strauss and Mozart at the Theater an der Wien, under the expert hand of Josef Krips, later Karajan and Furtwängler. As she recalls, "We were very fortunate, for at that time these conductors rehearsed us at the piano every day, even after the premiere, before every performance. We were always working on ensembles and tempos. These were days of great performances." In Milan, at La Scala after 1948, she experienced the same fanatacism for work with Victor De Sabata, who encouraged her to lend a more Italianate sound, more vibrato, to her instrument. As a leading Mozart stylist, she was chosen in 1951 to create the role of Anne Truelove in Stravinsky's *The Rake's Progress*—the composer's homage to classical opera.

Throughout Europe and America Schwarzkopf became the standard in those things which she did best, perhaps better than anyone else in her time. She concentrated on words and meaning, on coloration, on finding that exacting balance between heart and mind, on giving her public new emotional experiences through her singing. This is what made her Marschallin the definitive interpretation of the 1950s and '60s, for it is the one opera role closest to lieder in its intimacy and detail. "Here you paint with the same fine brush you use in recital," she has observed. And paint Elisabeth Schwarzkopf did. Now she is passing on her coloristic skills through master classes, and through her recordings—of her major roles, lieder, the "champagne" operettas and Strauss's Four Last Songs—we keep relishing this highly refined art of Elisabeth Schwarzkopf.

Placido Domingo

Ubiquitous and inexhausible, Placido Domingo is the marathon man of opera. In some twenty years he has sung far more performances than most singers do in an entire lifetime. He dominates the recording market, and he has made more television appearances in opera than any other singer of his day. He wants to reach people, "to be known by many people in my own time." And he keeps running, defying the doomsayers who predicted he would quickly burn himself out. He thrives on a hectic schedule, on doing roles that don't come easily, on courting fate, on wanting to be the one who sings the most. In ten years he has sung some 1,600 performances in 80 operas—all jotted down in little green books (green for hope). He jets all over the world, often mixing strenuous live performances with recording sessions, sometimes not even in the same city.

Close friends say this drive comes from Domingo's mother and father, who brought their zarzuela company from Spain to Mexico when Domingo was a child. They sang all the time, his mother a celebrated soprano, his father a baritone. They loved to sing, and Domingo's mother had to be brought home from the theater to give birth. His father is from Aragon, his mother from the Basque country, and they dreamed of having their son become a singer. He first played the piano and then sang as a baritone in zarzuelas, but he was determined to bring his voice up to the tenor range. He had help from his teacher, Carlo Morelli, then his wife, Marta (a singer herself), and

a colleague, baritone Franco Iglesias. Domingo and Marta left Mexico in 1962 for a stint with the Israel National Opera, where he solidified his technique and found the right way to sing, with breath support and proper use of the diaphragm, gaining security in the upper register. Today, he observes, "Vocally now, more or less everything is in place, if I am rested and healthy." As for the notorious high C, which he more often than not avoids in performance, he insists, "No, it's not a frustration. I don't deny I would be happy if I had an easy high C. But I am in great company, because the greatest of all, Caruso, was not happy with his high C and sang it little. Also Gigli." He has said he takes the note in *Manon Lescaut, Un Ballo in Maschera, Turandot,* and *Otello,* but not in *La Bohème, Il Trovatore,* and *Faust*—the decision based on the approach to the top tone and the general tessitura of the passage. "It is not such a big thing for me, because I don't base my singing on just one note." His voice has the weight and heft of a dramatic tenor, coming from its baritone origins, as well as a timbre that buzzes with electricity, slightly covered, but ringing in the true Italian tradition.

Although Domingo had come to America after his Israel experience and various assignments in Mexico, his big breakthrough happened with the world premiere of Alberto Ginastera's *Don Rodrigo,* which opened the New York City Opera's new home at Lincoln Center in 1966. He was unknown and scored a triumph in a tremendously difficult role. Two years later he was at the Metropolitan as Maurizio in *Adriana Lecouvreur.* Domingo is a singer whose seriousness, intelligence, and immaculate musicianship make him a conductor's and director's dream. He has the strength of a bull and is always prepared. Color is the key to the way he looks at repertory. Domingo has been famous for not concentrating on a handful of roles or even a certain repertory; instead, he has tried almost everything. "It is better to have variety," he says simply, "and I learn very fast. I know my voice better than anyone. I keep it lighter every day through coloring. If I do Otello, it has to have a baritone color, dark and thick. I sing with my voice, and only the color changes." Naysayers predicted doom when Domingo, still a far throw from forty, decided to try his first Otello. Now he has sung the role everywhere, coming through the test with flying colors. "I proved I was not doing anything crazy. I'm glad I've proved everyone wrong." The living proof is that he can mix Alfredo in *La Traviata,* Des Grieux in *Manon Lescaut,* Riccardo in *Un Ballo in Maschera,* Don José in *Carmen,* and Hoffmann in *Les Contes d'Hoffmann* with Otello, and to startling effect as well as ease.

Domingo is married and the father of three boys. He is conducting more and more, learning from the conductors with whom he regularly works—James Levine, Carlos Kleiber, Zubin Mehta, Carlo Maria Giulini. He is trying more vocal concerts —an area from which he shied for years—and he would like to promote zarzuelas and Latin American music everywhere. He plays golf, tennis, and soccer. He's talking about a small theater with a school to train young singers. Placido Domingo is protean in his energy, a restless long-distance runner.

Maria Callas

Maria Callas and Giuseppe di Stefano

I f ever the world of opera has produced a name with enduring household familiarity around the globe, it is that of Maria Callas. When the great singer died—suddenly, tragically—in 1977 in Paris, it was international news. Despite a relatively short career, she already belonged to the ages, her legendary status firmly established. Any singer worth his or her salt acknowledges that Callas reshaped opera. Her glittering years in the 1950s, centering on Milan's La Scala, were greeted as a new golden age, with Callas as its queen. Together with directors Luchino Visconti and Franco Zeffirelli and conductors Victor De Sabata and Carlo Maria Giulini, she thrust opera into the forefront. Every Callas performance became an event, and the pressures attendant on such close scrutiny undoubtedly led to her early demise and retirement from the stage.

Originally heavy and awkward, but possessed of a powerful and fascinating soprano voice, she made herself thin and glamorous through sheer determination. She learned to act as few others could, reigning supreme in the classic roles: Bellini's Norma, Donizetti's Anna Bolena and Lucia di Lammermoor, Cherubini's Medea, among others, figures brought to life by a stylized approach, a nobility of carriage, a commanding gesture of the arm, a quietly intense concentration. To a repertory often dominated by light, birdlike voices she brought a whole new dimension with her strange, dark, often bottled-up colorations—most prominently as Lucia or Bellini's Amina in *La Sonnambula*. She built the upper extension of her voice through work with Elvira de Hildago, much as Guiditta Pasta and Maria Malibran had done in the early nineteenth century at the height of the bel canto era. In her best days, Callas commanded a broad, amazing range from the low mezzo territory to an exultant E-flat or E-natural above high C. The registers were not always superbly knit, and the sounds she emitted varied in quality, texture, and timbre—someone once said her voice was an acquired taste like Greek olives or feta cheese—but her approach linked her to the legendary sopranos of the past century, and with her studied acting style, Callas came to embody the heroines of that age.

Opera lovers often talk of an imperfect voice or technique, but at her peak there was little that Callas could not command, either from a natural gift or from what she forged by an iron will. Hers was a voice created by a desire to achieve and sing, a need to prove herself in the most fervent, heated way. Each night Callas came to the stage, a war seemed to be waged—within herself, between herself and the public and the critics, between herself and those who had slighted her along the way. Callas made news wherever she went: her feuds with general managers of opera houses, her historic walkout during the

opening-night *Norma* in Rome with the president of Italy in attendance, her separation from her husband, Meneghini, her alliance with Aristotle Onassis, her various returns to the stage, her reclusive life in Paris, and, finally, the lonely death. Her existence on the opera stage has been likened to a candle that quickly burns itself out, a fiercely bright but brief meteor in the sky—as if she had been put on this earth to blaze brilliantly for a few years and then vanish. One cannot deny her potent influence, the attention to the theatrical expression of opera that could never be the same once Callas had left her imprint. Someone once suggested that the three supreme figures of the opera in this century had names beginning with C—Caruso, Chaliapin, and Callas.

With Callas came a rebirth of the bel canto operas, many buried in the sands of time for more than a full century. It would be ridiculous to say that bel canto itself had died, for all through opera history up to World War II there had been those exponents of the Rossini–Donizetti–Bellini canon, but the works performed had boiled down to a precious few war horses. The reinstatement of *Anna Bolena* and *Poliuto* and *Il Pirata* and *Medea* proved major rediscoveries. Those who followed— Leyla Gencer, Montserrat Caballé, Renata Scotto, Beverly Sills— benefited from the door that had been reopened by Callas and her collaborators, who looked back to a miraculous age of singing and theater. Milan, then London, and finally Paris

became her principal theaters of operation on the Continent. Chicago held her on a pedestal for the first two glorious seasons of the then-new Lyric Opera. A dispute over a process server sent her to Dallas, where Lawrence Kelly and Nicola Rescigno were launching into a daring new venture in that Texas town. New York did not hear Callas at her best: her 1957 debut as Norma was not sung at her optimum, the audience antipathy having been fired by a *Time* cover story that week in which the singer denounced her mother and Renata Tebaldi, the diva's great rival. Callas's return to the Met in 1965 as Tosca—years after her well-publicized dispute with Rudolf Bing over repertory—came at a period of waning vocal resources, brought on in part by high living in café society. One wonders about the values of a woman who had everything in opera and remained unsatisfied. The glamorous life of ease, parties, and yachts drew this once-poor New York–born artist into its vortex.

For ten years or so Callas had reigned supreme. She helped rechart the vision of what opera can be. Her records, both commercial and pirated, are avidly collected and listened to, with endless fascination. The myriad colors of that voice linger in the mind, as does her poetic handling of the text. Chicago's Claudia Cassidy once likened her descending scales to autumn leaves drifting to the ground. Pathos and nobility cohabit in that voice. Callas took chances, she dared. We listened, and we still are listening.

Jessye Norman

When Jessye Norman moves out of the wings to center stage, she is more than a human being—she is a force, a vast reservoir of sound that emanates from the depths. And her tone pours forth like a cresting Pacific wave, a torrent filled with glittering and dark colorations. As a dramatic soprano she has been compared to Kirsten Flagstad and, closer to home, Helen Traubel, with whom she shares that comfortable middle range and a tendency to shortness at the very top of her voice. She can sing Sieglinde or Isolde or Elisabeth in *Tannhäuser,* but she is equally at home in the depths of Mahler songs. Because of her monumental proportions, stage performances in opera have been somewhat limited, especially in this age when physical appearance seems to have become as important as actual singing. Followers keep pondering the fate of Jessye Norman— opera star or concert singer, dramatic soprano or mezzo. She is a little of all these, growing, experimenting, deciding what best fits her stirring talents.

The soprano was born in Augusta, Georgia, and as a teenager entered the Marian Anderson competition in Philadelphia, after her high school friends had raised her train fare. She didn't win, but returning home she stopped off in Washington to sing for Carolyn Grant at Howard University. The teacher was so impressed that a full scholarship was quickly arranged. Then came one unsatisfactory semester at the Peabody Conservatory in Baltimore and a year and a half at the University of Michigan, where she worked with Pierre Bernac, a legendary master of the French chanson. It was there that her interest in the song literature was nurtured, from the classical lieder of Schubert, Schumann, Brahms, and Wolf to Poulenc and Satie. Winning the 1968 competition of the Bavarian Radio in Munich led to an engagement with the Deutsche Oper in Berlin under Intendant Egon See-Fehlner, and she made her debut in 1969 as Elisabeth in *Tannhäuser* after having never before been on the opera stage. Her repertory there came to include *Aida, L'Africana, Don Carlo,* and *Le Nozze di Figaro.* In 1970 she turned to Handel's *Debora* with Riccardo Muti at the Teatro Comunale in Florence, and in 1971 she sang in *Idomeneo* with Davis for the RAI in Rome and later opened the Maggio Musicale in Florence in *L'Africana.* La Scala and then the Royal Opera House at Covent Garden heard her too, the latter as Cassandra in *Les Troyens.* The only opera appearance she has made at home in America was as Aida at the Hollywood Bowl in Los Angeles. It has been her concert work, including acts and scenes from *Die Walküre* and *Tristan und Isolde* as well as her hauntingly beautiful song recitals, that has told the American public that hers is a spectacular voice with which to reckon. It is a special instrument, not quite filling any particular mold. In many ways it is the perfect Berlioz sound, a Falcon voice that encompasses the soprano range but with breadth and depth throughout the middle and lower registers. At a time when heroic voices seem to be an endangered species, Jessye Norman could lead the pack among those contending for such roles as Isolde and the Brünnhildes. Meanwhile, she belongs to Berlioz for a Met debut scheduled to take place in *Les Troyens* on opening night of the 1983–84 season.

Victoria de los Angeles

Barcelona-born Victoria de los Angeles has always seemed aptly named, for, truly, she descends from the angels both in the seraphic quality of her voice and in her glowing presence. Purity, luminosity, simplicity, tenderness sum up her person, her manner of singing. She has never failed to enchant wherever she has traveled around the world during her long career. And probably no more so than during the encores of her treasurable recitals when she graciously returns to the stage, guitar in hand, to play and sing "Adios Granada," a delicious moment in anyone's concert-going life. Her uncle, Angel, had taught de los Angeles to play the guitar as a child, and he left his instrument to her in his will. The singer is more than an angel, however; she is a true artist, one of extraordinary refinement, taste, perfection, ideals, and charisma. Her art extends from her most notable opera roles—Mimi, Madama Butterfly, Rosina, the *Figaro* Countess, Manon, Marguerite, Mélisande, Carmen—to the vast range of recital repertory in many languages and styles, of many periods. In fact, she counts among the few non-German singers openly accepted in German and Austrian concert halls singing Schubert, Schumann, Brahms, and Strauss. Wieland Wagner, that master director who could penetrate the very soul of a performer in order to mold a character ideally to his or her personality, saw the soprano's sweet, virginal, timeless quality when he invited her to Bayreuth in 1961 to sing Elisabeth in *Tannhäuser.* And how right he was! Those very qualities illuminated both her Eva in *Die Meistersinger* and her Elsa in *Lohengrin.* There is a naïveté—an innocence—about de los Angeles, a quality of manner that has stayed with her no matter how internationally celebrated she became. It is that lack of veneer, that girlish immediacy and instinctiveness of approach which lie at the heart of her ability to communicate with such directness. De los Angeles is serious, scrupulous, probing, intelligent, but never mannered or superficial. As with the greatest singers of any era, her song wells up from an inner source, rippling naturally, ravishing the ear—a veritable fresh-water stream whose sparkling lights and dark, mysterious depths delight, captivate, entrance.

Recitals and opera have coexisted side by side in the Spanish soprano's career, the former growing in importance as the years go by. De los Angeles made her concert debut at twenty in her native Barcelona in 1944, following this with a professional opera debut there in 1945 as the Countess in Mozart's *Le Nozze di Figaro.* Then, in 1947, she won the International Singing competition in Geneva, a prize that soon had her at the Paris Opera as Marguerite and Manon, at La Scala as Ariadne, at Covent Garden as Mimi, and finally at the Metropolitan Opera, again as Marguerite, the last three engagements all during the 1950–51 season. When about to make a debut in a major opera house, she always insisted on first giving a song recital in that city so as to become acquainted with her public, to introduce herself as Victoria de los Angeles the singer, the woman.

In all her work, the de los Angeles voice was often felt to be more a high mezzo-soprano than a true soprano because of the richness of its lower and middle registers. The singer could achieve the high tones all the way up to a D-natural above high C in Manon's gavotte, for instance, but at those altitudes vocal gold could sometimes turn to a baser kind of metal. Throughout her range, however, de los Angeles has always had a miraculous sense of pitch and rhythm, of aristocratic phrasing and identification with the fine points of any piece of music. The soprano is something of a purist, never producing a note or shaping a line simply to wow an audience, to make an extraneous effect; it must all be part of the whole, of the grand conception. Perhaps that is why she tended to prefer French opera to Italian, savoring the intimacy it demanded of the artist, its poetry and avoidance of showiness. Her handling of the French chansons of Debussy, Fauré, Berlioz, Ravel, Duparc, and Hahn shares the fragility, poignancy, and style she brings to the French roles onstage. Needless to say, the Spanish literature—songs and zarzuela arias—dominates her programs, and no de los Angeles recital is complete without a large dose of Falla, Granados, Obradors, and many others, the selection ranging back to the Middle Ages and forward to our own century—an astonishing legacy of song, gloriously handed down by the soprano. In this repertory she reveals the duality of the Spanish character, the duality of her own person: glitter and sadness, pride and vulnerability, patrician and earthy, flirtatious and remote. And never has this been more apparent than when she collaborated with her friend and sister Catalan, Alicia de Larrocha, for a sprinkling of historic recitals, in which the vocal and pianistic traditions of Spain flowered hand in hand. On those occasions Victoria de los Angeles seemed indeed to have been sent from Heaven, to become our Angel of Song.

Marilyn Horne

It's that simple: Marilyn Horne is probably the greatest singer in the world. If one talks of singing per se, of meeting head-on all the demands of the bel canto lexicon, she reigns supreme. Only Joan Sutherland, with whom she often collaborates, can equal her on this ground. When it comes to singing, and singing with the full battery of agility, trills, range, color, brilliance, legato, articulation, dynamics, Marilyn Horne is today's undisputed mistress, and for all we know a real throwback to the days when Rossini and his prima donnas ruled.

Marilyn Horne is likely at some point to talk about Pauline Viardot and Marietta Alboni, the two greatest contraltos of the nineteenth century. She feels an affinity for the former, who began as a soprano and later inspired Meyerbeer to write *Le Prophète*, and for the latter, who was Rossini's pet pupil and prima donna for his mezzo heroines. She's fascinated by those nineteenth-century ladies—their repertory, their style, how they produced their sound. She's read and learned and worked hard and long for the past quarter-century-plus, believing since she was a child that she had one thing, her voice—that people could take anything away from her but the voice, which is hers to care for and nurture.

She loves to talk about singing, analyzing, trading views, expressing amazement at hearing her own voice on records. She attempts to describe it: "It's this peculiar darkness of my voice with this gleam, this brightness. And then there's that dramatic thrust to it, a rhythmic thing that gives my singing its strength, its force. It's really hard to sort it out, and it took me a long time, especially when you consider that I've been singing all my life, since I was a little kid." And she loves to sing. You feel this when she walks onstage for a concert or an opera, or if you catch her on television. She communicates, or wants to communicate, with almost youthful eagerness. Singing is what she's been doing forever, and despite all the slings and arrows that have come her way, the mistakes, the wrong turns, the problems, the headaches, Marilyn Horne loves to sing—maybe now more than ever. She still has something of the precocious child about her, the high-school overachiever who always has her hand up first, who is full of beans, bright, open, vulnerable.

Marilyn Horne began as a soprano—"At eighteen my voice was like Judy Blegen's"—going to Gelsenkirchen in 1956 to sing Mimi in *La Bohème* and Minnie in *La Fanciulla del West*, returning home for Marie in *Wozzeck* with the San Francisco Opera. But her marriage to black conductor Henry Lewis changed all that. Just as her father in Bradford, Pennsylvania, had taken a commanding interest in her voice, followed by her teacher, William Vennard, in Los Angeles, so did Lewis begin to reexamine it, only to come up with the conclusion she was a mezzo and destined for bel canto. At one point she began flirting with soprano roles all over again, mainly Wagnerian parts, but long, hard soul-searching and coming to grips with her true talents led her back onto the true path. As she observes, "I'm a throwback to another age—a soprano with mezzo qualities, or a mezzo with soprano qualities." The mysteries of singing stay with her, but she knows where her absolute strengths lie: Bellini, Rossini, Handel, Vivaldi, Meyerbeer. Forays into Verdi have been met with more mixed reception. "I find that knowing what I know now about all the things I've sung, I can take a role like Tancredi or Italiana or Orlando, and I can get onstage and *play* with it. I can do anything I want, and that's got to tell me something. They're *absolutely* right for me."

The mezzo has come to realize that all the parts which were specialties of Alboni, parts written for her or which she sang, seem to suit her: Arsace in *Semiramide*, Tancredi, Malcolm in *La Donna del Lago*. "All the Rossini stuff, and I do know she was Rossini's favorite singer and he taught her voice. She remained his favorite and would come to visit, and he would always ask her to sing. We also know she got so fat she had to sing sitting down," and she roars with laughter. Rossini dubbed Alboni an "elephant who swallowed a nightingale." That's one comparison Marilyn Horne would like to avoid.

Critics heaped praise on Alboni because of her three-octave range, deep, full, mellow tone, organlike richness of volume, resemblance to a man's velvety tenor, clear and fluent articulation, immaculate precision and purity of intonation, and speed of execution, all of which apply to her amazing modern counterpart. Horne is intrigued by Manuel Garcia's theories and virtuoso exercises. At one time she tried to sound like Renata Tebaldi and Ebe Stignani. Rosa Ponselle became an inspiration via her records, because of her incredible line, the ring in the voice, the dark hues, the coloratura technique, and the purity of tone. In our own time, Marilyn Horne inhabits her own Golden Age.

José Carreras

Of all the tenor voices to come along in the past dozen and a half years or so, the most ravishing in timbre belongs to the Catalan tenor José Carreras. Its resemblance to the voice of his Italian predecessor Giuseppe di Stefano is uncanny—that same sunny, open quality, that emotional throb, that geniality of spirit, that flood of liquid tone. With the help of his already acclaimed countrywoman, Montserrat Caballé, Carreras hit the international scene with thundering impact. His performances at the New York City Opera beginning in 1972 proclaimed a major talent in our midst—and the world was hungry for just such a tenor, one with this kind of generous voice and boyish good looks to go with it, as well as an ingenuous, disarming manner onstage. The Caballé connection quickly brought him to sing in *Lucrezia Borgia, Luisa Miller, Maria Stuarda, Caterina Cornaro,* and *Adriana Lecouvreur* all over Europe.

Born in 1946 in Barcelona, he began piano and solfège lessons at eight, when he also saw his first opera at the Liceo— *Aida*—which unleashed an enthusiasm in him for this art form. At seventeen he started voice studies with Jaime Francisco Puig, but he studied chemistry too for three years, since his father owns a small chemical plant and insisted on it. He made his debut in Barcelona in 1970 and then won the Verdi competition in Parma before coming to New York. Covent Garden, Vienna, the Metropolitan, and La Scala followed in short order. Carreras emerged as the latest in a healthy line of contemporary Spanish tenors: Alfredo Kraus, Giacomo Aragall, and Placido Domingo among them. In fact, it was Kraus who predicted in the early 1970s that the young Carreras would be the next big tenor star. Herbert von Karajan took an interest in him, stretching his capabilities with the Verdi Requiem, *Don Carlo,* and eventually *Aida,* as well as the more predictable *La Bohème.* Carreras deems Karajan the greatest conductor of our time. "A man from another galaxy. I feel, and many of my colleagues think the same, that with Karajan, it is like having your father there, conducting for you. You feel incredible, as if 'He is following me the whole performance. I can do anything I want.' But the big secret is—and only a few conductors have the sensibility and intelligence to do this—that you are really following him. Only his magnetism makes you think that he is following you. He moves a single finger and you must give him everything you have inside you."

Today Carreras works with all the leading conductors and directors on the world's stages, trying to learn from them as well as going to the theater to watch his colleagues. He has confessed to being an inadequate actor—but one willing to learn. He feels he acquired a lot about the dramatic aspect of opera from his work with the New York City Opera, having arrived there as an inexperienced, provincial singer. "I learned the right way to approach music, attention to the composer's wishes, taste, style." He also built up his repertory: *Madama Butterfly, Lucia di Lammermoor, Tosca.*

He said early in his career he loves to listen to records— not to imitate, "just to luxuriate in beautiful singing. I greatly admire Bjoerling, who was such a complete artist. Being Latin myself, though, I feel instinctively drawn to the passionate expression of di Stefano." As with most tenors, he reveres Enrico Caruso, viewing him as a myth, "like Greta Garbo." But while he admires the incredible quality of the voice, he realizes that singing styles change over the years, and he deems only one tenor who would be modern enought to sing today: Aureliano Pertile, Toscanini's favorite tenor. "He respected more the music, respected what the composer wrote. He used not so much portamento, the cries, the sobs. A very honest interpretation always from Pertile, not seeking big applause."

José Carreras is forever busy, traveling, singing, recording, learning repertory. Observers are keeping tabs on him as he explores increasingly heavy, demanding roles, praying that the toll will not be felt in the quality of his singing. While Nemorino in *L'Elisir d'Amore* and Rodolfo in *La Bohème* are ideal, he has his eyes on Andrea Chénier and the mighty Verdi heroes. He brings an openness and a simplicity to his work—the honesty of one trying hard to please and to succeed. There is a refreshing modesty about him as he learns and hones his craft in the international spotlight. José Carreras is a meteor that we hope will burn brightly for decades to come.

Renata Tebaldi

For many Renata Tebaldi is the Madonna of opera. Through good times and bad, her performances have been met with a kind of religious awe, perhaps because she may be the last of the great old-style sopranos to emerge from Italy. Her tall, imposing, handsome persona announced that a prima donna had arrived, and even though she became more glamorized in her American years, her white alabaster skin and engulfing dignity always bespoke purity and reserve. In its heyday Tebaldi's soprano wafted truly angelic—a flood of golden, creamy sound that filled out a Verdi or Puccini line with majesty and allure, and, so important, it was identifiably hers alone. When she was onstage with Franco Corelli, the mighty Italian tenor of the late 1950s, 1960s, and 1970s, one knew that this was how the passionate Italian operas—*La Gioconda, Andrea Chénier, La Bohème, Tosca, Adriana Lecouvreur*—should sound. Their voices joined in an inexhaustible outpouring that left listeners dumbstruck by the pure opulence, thundering size, unbridled ardor—in other words, the very heart of these emotional works was exposed.

Tebaldi has long been part of a magical love affair between herself and her public. From the moment she stepped onstage, she embraced her audience with that famous open smile and her regal, commanding presence. Communication was immediate, undeniable. Critics vied to encapsulate her sound in

terms ranging from rich and warm to delicate, sumptuous, glowing, velvety, womanly—all virtues bound to capture an adoring public. But it was the combination of *all* these virtues that made Tebaldi unique, for she could peal forth in heroic resplendence or scale down to the most shimmering, ethereal pianissimo, always honoring the score with scrupulous care for dynamics. From her unusual early repertory—which included Rossini's Mathilde in *Guglielmo Tell* and Pamira in *L'Assedio di Corinto*, Handel's Cleopatra in *Giulio Cesare*, Spontini's *Olimpia*, and Amazily in *Fernando Cortez*—to her familiar Verdi and Puccini parts, she reveled in luxuriant sound, expansive phrasing, silken legato, finely turned portamenti, kaleidoscopic changes of light and dark. These trademarks extended from the lyrical Mimi in *La Bohème* to the dramatic La Gioconda and Minnie in *La Fanciulla del West*. Early in her career she had ventured into Wagnerian roles as well—Elisabeth in *Tannhäuser*, Elsa in *Lohengrin*, Eva in *Die Meistersinger*, all in Italian—yet what she will be remembered for are her quintessential Italian roles: Tosca, Manon Lescaut, Mimi, Madama Butterfly, Violetta, Desdemona, the *Forza* Leonora, La Gioconda, Adriana Lecouvreur.

Born on the Adriatic in Pesaro, hometown of Rossini, Renata Tebaldi studied at the Arrigo Boito Conservatory in Parma, deep in Verdi country, where she became a protégée of soprano Carmen Melis. The young singer made her professional debut as Elena in Boito's *Mefistofele* at Rovigo in 1944. Two years later she was chosen by a fellow Parmigiano, Arturo Toscanini, to participate in the concert that reopened La Scala in Milan after World War II—an event that launched her internationally. In 1950, on tour with La Scala, she made her debut at the Edinburgh Festival and Covent Garden, and in America Tebaldi first appeared with the San Francisco Opera. The following year she went to Paris in the Naples San Carlo Opera production of Verdi's *Giovanna d'Arco* and then sang at all the major houses of South America. Although contracts had been offered earlier, the soprano did not sing at the Metropolitan Opera until 1955, as Desdemona in *Otello,* a favorite role that ideally suited her personality. In 1963 she at last had the chance to perform her favorite part at the Met, Cilea's *Adriana Lecouvreur,* that "humble handmaid of creative genius"—a creed that seems to have governed both her art and her life. By the mid-1970s her career had come to a close, and she settled back, quietly and with dignity, in her native country.

No soprano coming after Renata Tebaldi has her unique qualities, particularly her legendary instrument. An age of thrilling grand-opera presence expired with her retirement. There had been hard days for Tebaldi, especially after her mother died and vocal crises forced her to withdraw temporarily from the stage to restudy technique. Tebaldi was born with a stupendous natural voice, but one hears a certain lack of technical finish even on her earliest recordings, especially in her approach to the higher notes. Some of her years in the theater found her in open battle with those notes, but all through her career the love of a faithful public spurred her on.

Renata Tebaldi and Franco Corelli

Leontyne Price

Her legion of recordings and performances may have dulled the impression of hearing Leontyne Price for the first time. Was it as a youthful Tosca on a 1955 NBC Opera telecast— or later as Pamina or as Lidoine in Poulenc's *Dialogues of the Carmelites,* all meltingly lyric? Was it that astonishing first Metropolitan Opera Saturday afternoon broadcast as Leonora in *Il Trovatore,* one that sent thousands out to the nearest record store to find her first complete opera recording—*Il Trovatore?* Was it an incomparably luxuriant "Chi il bel sogno di Doretta" (*La Rondine*) on what quickly became known affectionately as her "blue album" for RCA? Was it that taped broadcast from Salzburg with her mentor, Herbert von Karajan, challenging the heavens in a now legendary *Trovatore* with Giulietta Simionato, Franco Corelli, and Ettore Bastianini, and Price pure incandescence as she capped the "Miserere" with optional high C's? Was it as Liù at the Chicago Lyric, a radiant newcomer among the heavyweight Birgit Nilsson–Giuseppe di Stefano team for a hair-raising *Turandot?* Was it Donna Anna on either side of the Atlantic with that dark, rich outpouring for "Or sai che l'onore" and breathtaking measured trills in "Non mi dir"? What matters the exact occasion? They all remain engraved in the mind, as does perhaps her greatest moment of all, the Verdi Requiem, particularly when the Scala company came to North America in 1967, Karajan at the helm. It was sheer perfection, and the soprano's fierce religious beliefs, combined with her heaven-sent instrument, seemed to be all that Verdi had ever desired.

Leontyne Price brings something unique, something treasurable, something warm and pulsating into our musical lives. The technique remains sovereign, the voice a miracle in its cultivation. Her self-discipline when she is performing is a wonder; she enters her own self-imposed convent so that all her physical and musical faculties are in pristine condition for the stage. When she walks out on a bare platform, the place is suddenly suffused with a glow. She loves to sing, to share her prodigious gifts. The velvety, radiant voice, the passionate commitment, the hypnotic fervor of her singing rivet. That high vocal placement, God-given and in generous quantity, and that singular ability to spin a soaring tone to infinity beget wonder. Here and abroad she is in a heated affair between singer and public, reveling in that immediate audience response of concerts, that affinity for direct human contact—unlike others who must hide behind a character, a costume, theater mystery. It's no wonder that in recent years she's been prone to declare, "I'm in love with my own voice." She has every right to be.

Leontyne Price has had her good years and precious few bad times but has come through more stirring than ever. She has had her mind on career longevity, on choosing her repertory well, on giving her complete energies to the art of performing, never stinting. Not long ago when asked how it felt to arrive at that moment in life when one is given the accolade of "national monument," Leontyne laughed, with typical heartiness, and replied, "I just want to burst out singing!" That's what she has been doing for some thirty years now, much to the delight of the world, and she'll be doing much the same for a long time to come.

I n an era witnessing the demise of the old-fashioned diva, Leontyne Price is a comfort. More than that, she is authentic, a diva of the highest standing, a prima donna. Those words—*diva, prima donna*—can ring negatively of capricious temperament, of silly extravagances, of all show and no substance. But Leontyne Price reigns because she delivers; no one can claim to have been quite the same after having sat in an audience and watched her as she let that vibrant stream of pure gold fill a hall. It is molten lava, a voice of gorgeous substance that gains momentum, power, and glory as it sails upward to the magical high C.

Leontyne Price has filled many a hall and ravished many an ear since her first outings as Gershwin's Bess between 1953 and 1954—or even earlier in a Juilliard School *Falstaff,* where the seeds of her Verdi repertory were sown. Those who heard her knew she was destined for the top, and soon came that progression of international triumphs: San Francisco (1957), Vienna and London (1958), Salzburg and the Metropolitan (1960), and La Scala (1962). Marian Anderson had been a token gesture at the Met back in 1954 when she broke the color barrier to sing Ulrica in *Un Ballo in Maschera,* but Leontyne Price came to sing roles never before accepted by a white audience from a black soprano—Donna Anna in *Don Giovanni,* Leonora in *Il Trovatore,* Pamina in *The Magic Flute,* as well as the more expected Aida, a role that not only became a signature but her own personal statement about her people. In 1966 she made history by playing Cleopatra in Samuel Barber's *Antony and Cleopatra* to open the Met's new home at Lincoln Center. No woman could ask for more.

Sherrill Milnes

Bestriding the world as the all-American baritone, Sherrill Milnes is the latest in a grand line that includes Lawrence Tibbett, John Charles Thomas, Leonard Warren, Robert Merrill, Cornell MacNeil—not only Americans but Verdians to boot. Milnes's voice is big and burly, like his physical frame. He commands the stage with a swagger and an authority that make the ladies' hearts skip a beat. He exudes a sexuality, a machismo that is undeniable. He has specialized in Verdi, slowly building his repertory of those formidable parts that range from princes and counts and doges to jesters and bourgeois fathers. Playwright-critic George Bernard Shaw complained that Verdi kept the baritone voice banging away at the top third of the range, but here is where Milnes's strength lies. There's almost a hint that he could have switched over to the Heldentenor roles of Wagner, the Siegfrieds and Tannhäusers, had he wished. For his voice marches up and up to G, G-sharp, A, and even B-flat, right into the tenor domain, and securely, vibrantly. With the strongest of Otellos, Milnes as Iago can hold his own in the thundering "Si pel ciel" that brings down the curtain on Act II. His brilliant cabaletta as Miller in Act I of *Luisa Miller* literally made him a star at the Metropolitan in the late 1960s, and since then he has put his mark on the vast Verdi repertory: *Macbeth, Ernani, I Vespri Siciliani, Rigoletto, La Traviata, Don Carlo, Un Ballo in Maschera, Il Trovatore, Aida, La Forza del Destino, Boccanegra.*

All those noble, troubled, besieged figures are a long way from the Illinois farm where Milnes was born. His mother, a singer, pianist, choir director, and conductor, had always been active in her community, teaching voice as well as leading the choir. Milnes studied violin, piano, and voice, sang in choir each Sunday, and played and sang in high-school concerts. Eventually he went to Drake University and concentrated on voice, because his instrument had finally found its placement. At Northwestern University he began to sing with Margaret Hillis's Chicago Symphony Chorus. He was teaching school and doing radio commercials, having a bent for jazz. "You get a lot to like with M-a-r-l-b-o-r-o" was one, as was Schlitz, Kellogg's Corn Flakes, and Budweiser Beer. Opera workshop performances led to Boris Goldovsky's touring company—fifty-three Masettos in *Don Giovanni* on tour, plus two summers at Tanglewood, and more cross-country tours. In 1961 he bowed with Rosa Ponselle's Baltimore Civic Opera as Gérard in *Andrea Chénier.* This led to Pittsburgh, San Antonio, Houston, Cincinnati, and a debut in Milan at the Teatro Nuovo in *Il Barbiere di Siviglia,* preceding his New York City Opera debut as Valentin, followed by Figaro and the elder Germont. Then 1965 brought him to the Met in *Faust,* and from that moment he has literally reigned in the baritone slot—not only the Verdi canon but also *Don Giovanni, Pagliacci,*

Chénier, Pique Dame, Eugene Onegin, Lohengrin, Das Rheingold, and the world premiere of Levy's *Mourning Becomes Electra.* Europe has followed suit with acclaimed debuts in London, Salzburg, Milan, and elsewhere.

Milnes is conscious of his image, of building it and touching his audience. He keeps in prime physical condition with a gym in his apartment. He looks and acts the role of the dashing hero. He's conscious of timing in doing a new role, of ticket sales, of fees and publicity. "Part of being an opera singer," he has said, "is marketing a product. I sell a commercial product in the opera world. I sell a sound that is, by normal standards, a pleasant sound, not an offbeat one that requires an offbeat repertory. I can sing all the standard and French things. I simply try to do what dozens—no, hundreds—of baritones have done over the years, except that I try to do it better."

He believes in reaching the mass audience in his concerts by programming music with entertainment value. He feels the whole idea of opera's being accessible to only the privileged few is nonsense. "Music is primarily emotional, not intellectual. You don't have to have a degree to understand it; you can just let it wash over you, and your body will respond. But people think white tie, foreign language, gee, I don't dig that stuff. The traditional stance of the recitalist tends to keep the caste system in force. You know, 'Don't get too close, folks, my accompanist and I are in our own little world!' Or esoteric programming that distances performer from audience. It's suicide. I don't believe the sole purpose of music is to educate people, anyway. As a priority in my way of thinking, that is way down the line. Communication is the whole thing." And Milnes communicates. He brings people to their feet, applauding and cheering.

*Beverly Sills
and Sherill Milnes*

49

Shirley Verrett

At a point some years ago you could mention the name Shirley Verrett and know exactly what she was: a rich-voiced American mezzo-soprano who had begun her career with heavy emphasis on recitals and concerts but who eventually moved into the opera arena with increasing frequency and dynamic impact, performing all the standard roles: Carmen, Eboli in *Don Carlo*, Azucena in *Il Trovatore*, Amneris in *Aida*, Orfeo—then Neocle in *L'Assedio di Corinto*, Leonora in *La Favorita*, and Cassandra/Dido in *Les Troyens*. But over the years changes were in the wind. A singer whose voice had always had a strong top extension for a mezzo was now starting to make explorations into the soprano repertory, beginning with those roles considered crossovers: Lady Macbeth, Queen Elizabeth in *Maria Stuarda*, Adalgisa in *Norma*, the new Prioress in *Les Dialogues des Carmélites*. Soon she was attempting the impossible: she was Norma, the Druid goddess herself (the first artist in the history of the Metropolitan Opera ever to sing *both* roles in the house). And she was mixing this with forays as Dalila, a real contralto role, as well. She's also sung the title role of *Aida*, Amelia in *Un Ballo in Maschera*, Tosca, and Beethoven's Leonora/Fidelio. In an age that thrives on vocal specialization, Shirley Verrett became an enigma. What exactly is she? Soprano or mezzo? Eventually the critics and public came to realize this is a unique voice that fits where it fits, no matter how the composer labeled a role, harking back to the heyday of the early nineteenth century when singers just sang what suited or titillated them. She has looked at the repertory and found parts that suit her voice: the demands of the tessitura, both top and bottom—and her temperament, which blazes forth. One feels, as with many other contemporary singers, that her inspiration, her model is Maria Callas—for better or for worse.

While the singer had been concentrating on concerts early in her career, a Carmen at the Spoleto Festival in 1962 put her on the opera map, and soon thereafter she made debuts with the New York City Opera, the Royal Opera at Covent Garden, and the Metropolitan, with appearances in Moscow, Florence, and elsewhere scattered in between. Some of her greatest successes have taken place in Italy and London. She came to the Juilliard School in 1955 via Arthur Godfrey's "Talent Scouts" program, having grown up in New Orleans and then Southern California in a family of gifted amateur singers—her mother a soprano, her father a choir director. Opera was out of the picture because they were Seventh Day Adventists who frowned on the theater. But concert singing was fine, and the young Verrett looked to that American black pioneer Marian Anderson as an ideal. Still, the eternal lure of the theater brought her more and more into that circle as roles began to fascinate her—as well as the kind of stardom that comes with them. Her personality, too, seemed ripe for the stage, for she brings a statuesque intensity that rivets the attention. She is beautiful and magnetic, proud and elegant.

While she studied and won numerous awards as a mezzo, lingering at the back of her mind was the thought that her voice actually had soprano capabilities. Her first teacher, Anna Fitziu, had thought so from the beginning. Slowly, alone, she began working up the center of her instrument to handle the soprano roles and the endurance they require. Her system of vocalizing stretched the voice upward to D or even E-flat above high C, giving her solidity at the C and D-flat. She has managed to break many rules, to be unorthodox, iconoclastic. People have shaken their heads, wondering what this kind of singer is all about as she proceeded to abolish established vocal categories.

Shirley Verrett began her singing life with an arresting emotional sincerity, an honesty, a desire to communicate that swept her listeners into her heated sphere. Her work was deep, coming from that inner wellspring that speaks from the soul. The aura of success brought a certain grandeur to her persona, a sense of the diva. And yet she has never settled into any format, any predictable routine. She remains inquisitive, restless, on the lookout for new experiences. Summing up her artistic personality, she says, "What any artist must do is gather knowledge and apply it to whatever role he or she is singing. One's life experience must enter any role, and the vocal resources must be used as intelligently as possible. After all, that's what being an opera singer is really all about!" Shirley Verrett combines her career with being a wife and mother, far removed from the hoopla of stardom. She's a bit of a mystery, determined, serious. She makes her own rules. Shirley Verrett is a set of variations on an enigma.

Luciano Pavarotti

Since Luciano Pavarotti first came to the fore in the mid-1960s his career has just kept ballooning, achieving the legendary status that few singers in this century, or of all time, have known. Pavarotti is a household word across the world, even with people who can't tell the difference between *Aida* and *La Bohème*. Born in Modena, Italy, he has succeeded in touching millions of people through his performances, recordings, television appearances, film, book, and personal appearances. Pavarotti has reached out, just the way he reaches out to embrace his public during a recital or concert, or in a curtain call after the opera. Pavarotti is the singer nonpareil, the gastronome and dieter extraordinaire, the comedian, the entertainer, the personality, the oversized creature with the white handkerchief as his security blanket, the bon vivant who plays tennis, rides, paints, swims, and heads a family. He's son and father, living life to the hilt.

That's the key to Pavarotti—enjoying life with gusto. That's what comes out of his singing, what brings sold-out houses

to their feet shouting after recitals and opera. He gives and he shares, and everyone around him talks of his generosity, his big heart. "The pleasure of the profession," he says, " is the human warmth around me, the public out there. I always had this, even before I was a singer. As a child too, I was the same—I was never home but at other houses always talking and joking. My life is full of people, generally good friends. I decide to spend my life with friends. I am a singer of success, and I am enthusiastic of the job I do and enthusiastic of life. I love people. This is an incredible and beautiful thing in life, to be kissed by God. If I am kissed by God, I thank him by doing my best. After the performance, the most beautiful thing is to remain one hour after to talk. These people come from all over, and they are in love with the art of Luciano Pavarotti."

Life was hard for the young Pavarotti, and he vividly remembers the war years in and around Modena, with the sounds of bombs falling. The family was poor, his father a baker of bread. At twelve Pavarotti fell ill with a near-fatal blood infection for a full twenty-four hours. "I saw death in front of me," he recalled years later. At the height of his career he was in a frightening plane crash at Milan's airport. "I want to tell everybody now why I am so enthusiastic of life. Life is good, even if there is trouble. I have seen what it is like to die. I am enthusiastic and optimistic and do all I do with all my heart. I am still simple. I am not complicated. I love life and put the world in the past and future—it's a big view of the world but by a simple, true, honest person."

Pavarotti's father is also a tenor, and the son remembers music in his life from childhood, especially records by Caruso, Gigli, Schipa, Pertile, and Bjoerling. After studies and beginnings in Italy, the tenor got his big start in England (at the Glyndebourne Festival) and Ireland, then in Australia with Joan Sutherland's touring company. He explains this with the familiar proverb that a prophet is without honor in his homeland. "To become someone in Italy, you have to go elsewhere. Then they kiss your feet, even if they are stinking, when you come back."

While Pavarotti sings all over the globe, America has become the focus of his operations, what with seasons at the Metropolitan, Chicago, and San Francisco, as well as jam-packed recital tours from coast to coast as he brings his familiar voice and figure to places that have never seen a live opera.

The 1967 season found him traveling with La Scala to Montreal's Expo 67 in Bellini's *I Capuletti e i Montecchi* with Renata Scotto and Giacomo Aragall—the young, thrilling, melliflous tenor as Tebaldo bore watching. In 1968 in New York he scored a success at his Metropolitan debut as Rodolfo in *La Bohème*, his perennial debut role. But it took nine high C's in

Donizetti's *La Fille du Régiment* in 1972 to put the official seal on the Pavarotti legend. Dubbed "King of the High C's," he has never looked back. Nemorino in *L'Elisir d'Amore* is close to his heart, to his peasant origins. He bumbles onstage, shy, flirtatious, adorable. At the other end of the specturm is Riccardo in *Un Ballo in Maschera:* courtly, handsome, serious, vocally the perfect blend of light and dark, what the Italians call chiaroscuro. From the high-flying Arturo in *I Puritani* and Ferrando in *La Favorita* he has marched on to Enzo in *La Gioconda,* Cavaradossi in *Tosca,* Radames in *Aida.*

Pavarotti constantly talks of his vocal cords, his throat, being "kissed by God," and in his case this must have been true. The tenor was born with a voice of natural sweetness and a naturally high placement that, at its best, makes singing seem almost an extension of the speaking voice—enhanced by his sensitive handling of the Italian language, through which he makes the music "speak." While not a robust voice, its superb head resonance, focused tone, and innate quality easily project to the last row of the theater. Pavarotti offers nothing of the raw animal excitement of a Corelli or a Del Monaco, but rather a honeyed, beguiling, golden quality that endears him to the listener. He seems born for the stratosphere and liquid legato of bel canto. With age and expansion of his repertory has come the patina of heft and darkness added to the basic sound, as well as a certain sense of the strenuous as the singer produces that flood of brilliant tone.

Pavarotti's voice glows like pure Italian sunshine, like clear, vibrant light glittering on the sea. Its sound is meltingly dulcet, natural, sexy, heady. The man's spirit is generous, expansive, thrilling. Onstage, he embraces his hyper public, draws them to him. He feeds on the adulation, applause, passion flowing across the footlights in both directions. The audience cannot get enough of this seductive man. He exudes waves of charm, and his need to communicate knows no bounds. The aria, the performance ends. Pavarotti's mouth falls open, his eyes droop, he flings his arms outward to his public. "Love me, love me," he seems to be saying, even insisting. "I've given you my blood, my sweat." And so he has.

Renata Scotto

Performing, singing are life and breath to Renata Scotto. Her total commitment to a role, to a score carries astonishing thrust. There is a fierceness in her performing that some observers find threatening, that causes her to be considered "controversial"—an artist whose work is forever hotly debated.

While Renata Scotto reigned as undisputed star of La Scala for over a decade, in the wake of Maria Callas and Renata Tebaldi, her American career was at first a series of frustrations and disappearances, culminating in her ultimately becoming prima donna of the Metropolitan Opera from the mid-1970s onward. In the early 1960s she arrived, with advance hoopla, at Chicago's Lyric Opera. Then came her Met debut in October 1965 in one of her most celebrated roles, Madama Butterfly, a successor to such renowned Cio-Cio-Sans as Albanese, Kirsten, de los Angeles, Stella, Tebaldi, and Price. Some found Scotto's voice unpleasant, not conventionally pretty; some found her acting almost harsh in its effect. But others recognized and heralded that spark of musical-theatrical genius granted to only a few performers. This impression was intensified when Scotto sang a superbly expressive, technically flawless Lucia di Lammermoor and an enchanting Adina in *L'Elisir d'Amore*.

But her Met years tended to be sporadic: a definitive Gilda in *Rigoletto*, a mesmerizing Violetta, more Lucias and Adinas, a striking revival of *La Sonnambula* (it was Amina that brought her to worldwide fame in 1957 when she replaced Callas

with the visiting Scala company at the Edinburgh Festival). Two pregnancies interrupted her career, but more disruptive was the seeming indifference of Met general manager Rudolf Bing. Meanwhile, Scotto's career continued to flourish in Italy with opening nights and ten new productions at La Scala, plus major revivals of rare works all over her native land. The breakthrough at the Met came in October 1974, when she returned to sing Elena in *I Vespri Siciliani*. Scotto proved electrifying, and James Levine, in the pit, instantly recognized her dramatic possibilities.

The cornerstone of Renata Scotto's art lies in a goal she continually reiterates: the necessity to "say something" in her singing. Zinka Milanov put it this way: "I like her vocal message." As a singer Scotto transcends mere singing or vocalizing, turning everything into dramatic utterance. She is the mistress of recitative in bel canto opera, and her sense of phrasing, of coloring each word, of accentuation and legato is a lesson in operatic art at a time when merely well-drilled, well-schooled, cool, charmless, increasingly mannered singing is becoming the norm. Scotto may often appear calculated in the impact she delivers, but that is how she has mastered and probed an aria or role. Onstage the spontaneity of creating something before the public becomes hypnotic, whether it be from Bellini, Verdi,

Puccini. It is a matter of achieving balance between technical control and emotional outpouring. It is one of those gifts beyond analysis or description. Scotto inhabits her own little world onstage, often oblivious to colleagues, but the audience is brought with her into that private world, full of magic and drama. As she sees it, "Onstage I feel to be a different person, but I don't forget to control the voice. It is difficult to find the balance, but you do it before in the rehearsal and in preparing. So onstage it is only a pleasure, a joy."

Born in 1934 in Savona on the Ligurian coast of the Italian Riviera, she moved at sixteen to Milan, where she stayed with Canossian nuns in a convent. Later she studied with the famous Spanish teacher Mercedes Llopart, who discovered the remarkable facility of the girl's upper register. Early in 1953, at nineteen, she sang "Sempre libera" in a young artists' competition, won it, and made her debut as Violetta at the Teatro Nuovo. The next season she joined La Scala to sing Walter in Catalani's *La Wally,* conducted by Giulini, with Tebaldi and Del Monaco.

Talking about her unmistakably inborn talent for singing, Scotto says openly, "With me it is inside, this *talento,* and no one can teach it to you. If you don't have it, you can't learn it. You can learn to sing and move, but that talent is still missing. I had it from the start." After Llopart strengthened her technique through the bel canto of Donizetti and Bellini, that repertory gave Scotto her finest moments. Later she began dropping these roles as her voice started to change, becoming darker, more dramatic, less free at the top. For some years she continued the lighter repertory of *Lucia, Sonnambula, I Capuletti e i Montecchi,* thus keeping her voice light. Then she added *I Lombardi* and *I Vespri Siciliani,* in which she began to produce more quantity of voice while maintaining her flexible technique throughout the range. More recently verismo operas have become increasingly important in her repertory.

Since the beginning of Renata Scotto's international career, people have wondered what she is all about. She seems to break the conventional rules and get away with it. She sang leggiero roles dramatically, and then kept adding heavier and heavier parts, juxtaposing the purity of bel canto with the more powerful Verdi and the passionate verismo. Few singers have done this and survived the rigors. But from the start, she would tell interviewers, "I am a soprano and nothing else," harking back to the nineteenth-century divas who sang the full repertory, and more recently to Maria Callas. Scotto was just a beginner in Milan when Callas enjoyed her heyday at La Scala, and the younger singer absorbed much of what she saw and heard. Compare recordings of the same aria and notice how the sopranos share that darkly covered tone, the care for words, the impulse for generous and meaningful phrasing, the concentration and focus of intent. Like Callas too, Scotto has a voice that not everybody finds ravishing on initial hearing; it's an acquired taste, and some never succumb to its wonders. There is a unique timbre, a metallic edge, a tendency to shrillness at the top and to wobble under pressure—qualities that in both artists seemed to increase with the passage of time.

The artist keeps adjusting her acting style, always refining and honing. She has forged her way without salvos from some critics, many of whom favor a safer, more predictable singer. Scotto remains on the tightrope, taking chances, forcing the listener to the edge of the seat not only in dramatic fervor but in vocal daring as well. She sums up: "I love the music. For me, the theater and music are unbelievably fantastic, and onstage it is a great happiness to perform and sing. Singing and performing— that is the greatest sensation!"

Mirella Freni

Talking about Mirella Freni, one uses the word *beloved*, for as with Lucrezia Bori or Licia Albanese or Victoria de los Angeles, the public takes Miss Freni to its bosom with a strong sense of protectiveness and love. In roles such as Mimi in *La Bohème*, Susanna in Mozart's *Le Nozze di Figaro*, Desdemona in *Otello*, Micaela in *Carmen*, Marguerite in *Faust*, she plays those sympathetic girls one instinctively wants to thrive, not die or be destroyed. The Freni career has bounded from one triumph to another at Covent Garden, Paris, La Scala, Hamburg, Salzburg, the Metropolitan, San Francisco, everywhere. The soprano seems to have found the key to the kind of career that makes an indelible impression: being the best in several roles—in her case first making a mark with Mimi, Susanna, Marguerite, Micaela, then slowly adding more dramatic repertory with Desdemona, Elisabetta in *Don Carlo*, Amelia in *Simon Boccanegra*, and Aida. The healthy lyric soprano has matured, adding weight, substance, and color. In her quiet, unassuming way she has met an extraordinary series of challenges over these years, without distorting the soft, sweet but penetrating timbre and delicate vocal palette.

One of the principal factors in shaping the Freni career has been Herbert von Karajan, with whom the singer has worked annually at Salzburg as well as in the recording studio and elsewhere. His potent influence came with the now historic *La Bohème* staged at La Scala in 1963, directed and designed by Franco Zeffirelli in unforgettable fashion. Later it was repeated in Vienna and Salzburg and made into a film. "We are very close," the soprano notes, "and it is strange, because you have

something with some people. With us it is almost psychic or telepathic, the understanding of us two. Things happen if we don't speak, we are together. And this happens immediately with us. We never have any problems. He likes always the beautiful aesthetic sound and the line—this is special for him, and I like it too. He loves me for this reason, because we do music the same way. Karajan wants always piano, even pianissimo, but with tension. Legato with tension. This is beautiful, but it is harder, not easier to sing."

As a result of Karajan's prodding and cajoling, Freni began to mix Susanna with Desdemona, Mimi with Elisabetta, a rare conjunction of repertory for her brand of lyric soprano. In 1970, for instance, when Karajan conducted and directed his new *Otello* at Salzburg, Freni emerged the Desdemona of one's dreams—young, radiant, vibrant with life, strong but vulnerable, innocently childlike, a victim in the grip of Jon Vickers's cobra Moor. Many came to scoff at the lyric soprano's bold entry into the more dramatic arena, but they scoffed no more once the curtain had fallen, and Karajan himself told her he had waited forty years to hear such a Desdemona. Still, Freni has moved cautiously, believing at first she cannot do a role, even though Karajan is convinced. She has been careful, not wanting to destroy the basic quality of her voice. She is worried, fearful, but she studies and prepares in a serious manner, putting new parts into her throat. "I sing these roles in my way, in a lyric way, with my voice, my personality," she explains.

Freni has been truly blessed over the years, working with the major conductors and stage directors, each guiding and urging her on—Karajan, Solti, Abbado, Giulini on the musical side, Barrault, Rennert, Visconti, Zeffirelli, Vilar, Ponnelle, Ronconi, Strehler, and Lavelli on the theatrical side. They have helped her stretch her talents to such works as Bellini's *Beatrice di Tenda* and *I Puritani*, Donizetti's *La Fille du Régiment*, and Tchaikovsky's *Eugene Onegin*.

Mirella Freni was born in Modena, where she and Luciano Pavarotti shared the same wet nurse while their mothers worked together in a cigar factory. Her grandmother had been a well-known singer of the twenties, Valentina Bartomesi. When Mirella entered a competition at a young age, the legendary Beniamino Gigli was a judge and told her, "You must be careful. You are young, and don't force your voice. Child prodigies often stay only that." She made her stage debut at twenty as Micaela in *Carmen* at Modena, after studies with Ettore Campogalliani at Mantua. For a while she stopped when her daughter was born, but in 1958 she won the Vercelli competition and sang Mimi there. Slowly things began to happen in Italy, then at Glyndebourne and Covent Garden. She maintains that rare reputation in opera, one of having few problems with colleagues, remaining friendly, cooperative, hard-working, combining a modest, child-like quality with the aura of a diva, sure of herself but warm, outgoing. She sees herself with a typically Italian temperament. "Yes! Because I am crazy and *pigra* ['lazy'] and sympathetic." That is the word for Mirella Freni: *sympathetic*.

Alfredo Kraus

Patrician is the quality that permeates the art and life of Alfredo Kraus. The tenor commands a noble style, a princely way of singing and moving onstage. He is one of the handful of singers in modern times who have found their repertory and stuck to it: Ernesto in *Don Pasquale,* Arturo in *I Puritani,* Edgardo in *Lucia di Lammermoor,* the Duke in *Rigoletto,* Faust, Des Grieux in *Manon,* Werther, and Alfredo in *La Traviata*—and more recently Hoffmann in *Les Contes d'Hoffmann* and Roméo in *Roméo et Juliette,* all of which suit him like the proverbial glove. Bel canto and the lyric French style have given Kraus's career its definition, its impetus, its distinction, its long-run success. He is a stylist, a serious artist, a man of purpose, and he knows his worth. He sings some fifty performances a season within this prescribed repertory, commanding top fees wherever he goes. He carefully plans his season, leaving sufficient days between performances, never running back and forth between cities to fulfill dates. Kraus recalls another age, a more settled time when singers arrived for a season, rested, ready to work, and Kraus consistently produces at the top of his form.

The tenor's voice has never been to all tastes, for it lacks conventional beauty—that robustness or Italianate throb. It is Mediterranean without a doubt, but of limited size, a bit metallic and wiry. But through his technical development, he has made it miraculously equalized throughout the registers, bright in color, supple in its ability to flow in a phrase, and astonishing in the tones where most tenors never dare ascend: C-sharp, D, and even up to an E-flat above high C. He has often been compared to the tenor whom he most admires, Tito Schipa. Kraus has observed, "With not one great quality, he made an extraordinary career. You can only call it genius. Schipa had a small voice, no top, just a nice middle, but it is unbelievable within this range what fantastic things he could do. Perhaps he had to be an artist because of his limitations, but even with a big voice you should be an artist."

And an artist is the right appellation for Alfredo Kraus. Born in the Canary Islands to parents of Spanish and Viennese background, he first became an industrial engineer before studying in Italy with Mercedes Llopart and making his debut in 1956 at Cairo—for an impresario who insisted he do both *Rigoletto* and *Tosca*. He has strenuously stayed away from the temptations of bigger repertory: *La Bohème, Tosca, Madama Butterfly, Andrea Chénier.* He has observed that a singer is like a boxer or weight lifter. If one tries to lift more than he can support, or if a boxer fights with someone heavier than he is, he will lose. "A singer can support only a role as heavy as his voice." Concerning roles, he is aware of the weight, the thickness of the orchestra, over which the singer must project and push his voice. Kraus projects, never pushes. He makes a lot of sense, believing that if a singer is in a repertory that is good from him, and he is considered one of the best in that repertory—why change? He feels sure and comfortable in what he sings. Why should he take unnecessary risks? From his early vocal studies he found a musical and technical base from which he has never veered in the intervening quarter-century. He told the Italian critic Rodolfo Celletti: "The stage forms the artist but ruins the singer. And I, by profession, am a singer. To be a singer you need a technical knowledge that you cannot have at twenty or even twenty-five. Technique is the basis of everything. You cannot be a singer if you are not a vocal technician, and you cannot be a good artist unless you are also a good singer." Celletti observed that, on the other hand, most tenors concentrate on natural qualities and an ability to improvise, while "the character [Kraus] habitually portrays…suits not only his voice but his elegant appearance, and his stylized stage movements, as well as his phrasing—subtle, highly musical, totally devoid of coarse emphasis and effects. It is difficult to imagine Kraus portraying a character who does not wear sumptuous costumes and whose language is not noble and in a certain sense idealized, because the smooth gentleness of his singing, the elegance of his phrasing, and his good stage looks make Kraus the only *grand seigneur* tenor of our time." With a prevailing sense of pride, good sense, wisdom, love of music, and respect for his art and profession, Kraus is a refreshing throwback to more princely times.

Beverly Sills

The impact of Beverly Sills on the American consciousness can never and probably will never be measured to its fullest. It happened over a fourteen-year period, before which Sills had been just another American singer trudging here and there for engagements. For years she was part of the adventurous New York City Opera ensemble, having auditioned there more than a half-dozen times before she was finally accepted for a debut as Rosalinda in *Die Fledermaus.* Her most prominent role came to be Baby Doe in Douglas Moore's American classic, *The Ballad of Baby Doe,* although she had not created it in its locale, Central City, Colorado, in the late 1950s. But came that fabled night in 1966 when she set off skyrockets as Cleopatra in Handel's *Giulio Cesare,* and the world of opera, the fate of Beverly Sills were forever altered. A series of new productions at her home theater—*Manon, Le Coq d'Or, Lucia di Lammermoor, Roberto Devereux, I Puritani, Maria Stuarda, Anna Bolena, Faust*—emerged side by side with exposure in South America and then Europe, the ultimate achieved with her debut at Milan's La Scala in a new production of Rossini's *L'Assedio di Corinto,* which earned her the cover of *Newsweek.* London, Vienna, Berlin, Venice, Naples heard her, if fleetingly, for she kept the bulk of her career close to home to be with her husband and children. In October 1980 she rang down the curtain on it all with a gala evening, almost twenty-five years to the day of her City Opera debut. It rounded things off nicely, and never let it be said that the soprano is not a smart lady, one who knows just how things ought to go. But disappear from the opera scene? Hardly. She became the new director of that company.

The soprano had always declared she'd rather have ten exciting years on the stage than twenty bland ones, and she did in that post-*Cesare* explosion. Those years were spent in a whirl of activity onstage and in the recording studio. She traveled the country top to bottom, coast to coast, singing recitals and concerts, and she became a celebrity through massive television exposure. Her combination of warmth, humor, earthiness, frankness, and good cheer—plus the voice, its bright, pale-gold color, its astonishing range and agility, and the wit and deep feeling of the delivery—captivated people who may not have had a shred of interest in opera. At one point the Metropolitan reported people were coming up to the box office asking for tickets to "the next Sills show."

She possesses a hard-to-define persona. Outside it's all sunshine, good humor, bubbles, smiles, a way of finding the right touch of lightness to deal with almost anything. Still, this is a woman of power, ambition, and standing—she's generous, yet aware of exactly who she is. She wants things smooth, uncontroversial, harmonious, at least on the surface. "It's not my style to be at each other," she states. She believes she can accomplish a great deal with a big grin, even though there are those who find it Pollyanna-ish. She's a confessed workaholic. "It comes from my father, who died when I was twenty," says the Brooklyn-born Sills. "My mother is pink-cheeked and easygoing, and she only gave us the dream. My father had energy and a good strong temper. He was a joyful man. My younger brother has it—he and I are movers." Her accomplishments have brought pride to the girl who once knew hard times, who met a good deal of opposition and disinterest, who worked and climbed with true grit, who at a crucial time in her life used singing as an escape from personal tragedies, who learned to sing for pure pleasure and not just to build a career, and who probably never dreamed of the kind of wealth and réclame she has amassed from this superstar career.

Now Beverly Sills is running her company, a full-time job of administering, casting, negotiating with unions, auditioning, fund-raising, shepherding, encouraging. Back in 1975, at the time of her Metropolitan Opera debut in *L'Assedio,* she was saying she'd like to be involved in the administration of a company. "I've spent most of my life in one, and I know the runnings and could be helpful." She's stressing its American qualities in singers, conductors, designers, directors, spirit. The company has grown from a shoestring operation of the 1950s to one seeking international status—and a budget to go with its image—and it has the presence of Beverly Sills, who put the City Opera on the world map. One thinks back on the career of this irresistible woman and the seventy roles she collected over the years. There's that red head bobbing as she bows, her expression a mixture of shy reticence and outright agreement with the audience acclamation. Looking back, she states openly, "There's no question, I pushed my voice. *Devereux* shortened my career by three or four years, and I knew it when I picked it. But I still go back to having those ten exciting years. Manon was made for me, but Queen Elizabeth I made my own." Does any one night stay in the memory? "Everyone expects me to say the first night of Cleopatra, but no, the first *Devereux* after Act II, when the audience stood up when I came out for a bow. I was used to it after a performance, but *not* in the middle of one." Beverly Sills broke all the rules and remains a unique American creation.

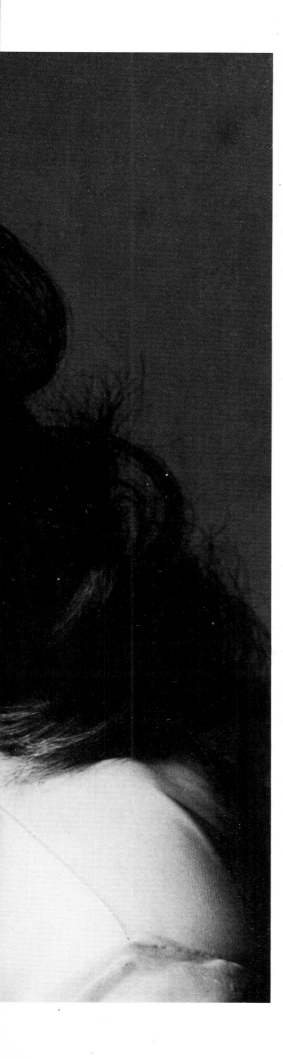

Frederica von Stade

Charismatic and mysterious, a real-life Mélisande in our midst, something ethereal and evanescent, Frederica von Stade has the kind of poignant, offbeat voice that touches the heart—almost like an oboe d'amore. Her style is simple, direct, moving, and deeply felt, yet never emotionally overladen. The singer is well-bred, aristocratic, like a sleek pedigreed filly, beautifully poised and vulnerable.

Von Stade grew up in a horsey New Jersey set, the daughter of a family with a background extending back to Colonial Connecticut and all that this entails—Social Register, polo, yachts, investments, private schools, convents. She went to the Mannes School in New York to learn to read music, "and I got into opera because it was the quickest way to a degree. I thought I'd never finish because I didn't have self-discipline." But there she met her longtime voice teacher, Sebastian Englebert. After graduation she set off for France to be a nanny and enrolled in a piano class at the École Mozart in Paris. There she heard her first recital given by Elisabeth Schwarzkopf at the Théâtre des Champs Élysées, "and I was enthralled." She had seen her first opera at fourteen, *Der Rosenkavalier* in Salzburg with Schwarzkopf and Christa Ludwig. But as a child, Flicka (as von Stade is affectionately known to almost everybody) had one idol, Ethel Merman, whom she saw ten times in a revival of *Annie Get Your Gun*.

With relatively little experience, von Stade arrived at the Metropolitan in 1970, first in small roles but soon moving up to Hansel, Stephano in *Roméo et Juliette*, Nicklaus in *Les Contes d'Hoffmann*, and Siebel in *Faust*. The opening of Rolf Liebermann's starry regime at the Paris Opera in 1973 gave her career its international impetus, for her Cherubino in Giorgio Strehler's celebrated staging of *Le Nozzi di Figaro* became the talk of Europe. She has sung at Glyndebourne, London, Salzburg, and most of the major capitals, while her Met career led to Rosina in *Il Barbiere di Siviglia*, Adalgisa in *Norma*, and Cherubino. Her repertory spans Monteverdi's *Il Ritorno d'Ulisse* (Penelope) to Pasatieri's *The Seagull* (she created the role of Nina in Houston), with Mélisande, the Rossini mezzo heroines, and more Mozart as regular specialties.

Von Stade's high lyric mezzo voice encompasses both the lower roles and certain soprano parts as well—an in-between role such as Massenet's Cendrillon suits her to a T. She believes that "a beautiful voice is just not enough; you want to be careful of expression and beauty of line and delivery....What I appreciate is a terrific artist *and* a beautiful voice, hand in hand." Along with striving for this, she has taken time off to have two children and then give them a sense of family life, whether it be in Europe or home in America. The singer plans and schedules carefully, with a certain air of independence. "I've never been consciously ambitious to be a star," she has said, "only musically, artistically...This art form is so valuable that it deserves that kind of ambition from everyone in it. A debut is thrilling, but if it's the wrong opera and circumstances, it is not necessarily a step forward. One should perform because it's right—to be as close to the best as you can offer the public." Frederica von Stade surveys her world with noblesse oblige.

Tatiana Troyanos

Mystery enshrouds Tatiana Troyanos. A reigning world singer, she is a veiled public figure. One knows little about her offstage life, her background, her private feelings. She is shy about interviews. Tall, voluptuous, dark, sable-haired, sexy, Tatiana Troyanos moves with ease between the sirens—Kundry, Venus, Giulietta—and the handsome pants roles—Octavian, the Composer, Hansel, Romeo, Giulio Cesare. At the Metropolitan Opera the mezzo-soprano has exhibited an astonishing breadth of repertory: Adalgisa in *Norma,* Brangäne in *Tristan und Isolde,* Charlotte in *Werther,* Amneris in *Aida,* Santuzza in *Cavalleria Rusticana,* Jocasta in *Oedipus Rex,* and Countess Geschwitz in *Lulu,* as well as her celebrated Strauss roles. Elsewhere she has explored such divers parts as Poppea in Monteverdi's *L'Incoronazione di Poppea,* Jane Seymour in *Anna Bolena,* Sextus in *La Clemenza di Tito,* and Judith in *Bluebeard's Castle.*

Tatiana Troyanos was born in New York City into a family of musical parents—her Greek father possessed a tenor voice, her German mother a coloratura soprano. She says she always wanted to sing, "but I was secretive about it. I had piano for seven years, so I knew I'd be in music some way." She sang in choruses, but managed to fail an opera course at the Juilliard School three times. Her interests were not yet focused, but her longtime teacher, Hans Heinz, began to influence her, opening up the door to opera as well as developing her instrument. She sang in the chorus of the original *Sound of Music* on Broadway and did summer stock in the New York area. Finally in 1964 she made it to the New York City Opera as an operatic novice.

In the mid-1960s Troyanos had been offered a Met contract but decided not to take it, sensing it would not lead to much. She felt she had to leave New York, where she had been gaining neither enough experience nor new repertory. In 1964, knowing little German, she auditioned for Rolf Liebermann of the Hamburg State Opera, and he masterminded her career for over a decade in Europe.

At the time she was a tall, somewhat gawky girl whose voice had not yet settled and found its core—someone with promise but definitely lacking polish, seasoning. She admits she went abroad with great expectations for the future, wanting to sing all the big parts like Carmen, Octavian, Eboli. But first she did small roles in modern operas. "I even did Suzuki, and I was terrible. I was so bad that the director, on the basis of that performance, said I had no chance in opera. I could do nothing right. But Liebermann was wise, because he wanted an ensemble with regular members, and he was right to have this. Finally, I did Carmen." Later she landed *Rosenkavalier* and *Nozze di Figaro* productions along with the premiere of Penderecki's *Devils of Loudun* (Hamburg, 1969). This led to Aix, Salzburg, Covent Garden, Munich, Vienna, and other theaters.

In Europe Troyanos went to the opera almost every night to listen, to observe, to learn. Leonie Rysanek made a tremendous impression with the sincerity and excitement she created in the theater. The mezzo says she was driven to have a career. "When I knew I had to develop, I was impatient and

driven. Now I feel less ambitious. I am not driven to everything anymore. You can't be. I'm grateful if a performance turns out reasonably well. Life goes on, even if you don't knock the world on its ear with your talent. I like competition too—in a healthy way. I love the fight and the struggle. Making music is a great thing to do, but I don't like all the pettiness that goes with it and the people you feel you can't trust."

Miss Troyanos longed to return home and reestablish her roots after the European stint that had transformed her into a major artist. The Metropolitan's James Levine convinced her to come back to New York. The rest is history.

Examining her voice, Troyanos notes its continual growth and the fact that with its strong upper extension there have been tempting offers to make forays into soprano repertory—

especially Leonore in *Fidelio*. She has powerful, easy high C's, which make singing Adalgisa in the original key (not transposed down) one of her specialties. But she thinks of herself as a lyric mezzo-soprano and avoids many of the more dramatic parts.

Music, she views, becomes a way of life because once the fight has been won, then it is necessary to maintain position, keep the talent in shape. "Music is a great part of my life. It has made me a disciplined person and grateful for what I have. I feel great if I sing well. I feel revived." Watching Miss Troyanos in performance, one is drawn to this strange, elusive creature who often seems to be warring with inner demons, relying on primal instincts that bespeak a cauldron of natural temperament, those flashes of light that ignite her style. Tatiana Troyanos is a seething fury out of Greek classical tragedy.

Christa Ludwig

One listens to Christa Ludwig in utter wonderment. The voice comes as an opulent gift of nature, an elemental force mated with formidable technique. In Brahms or Mahler songs she is a cello, her ripe tone glowing with deep, rich colorations, a mellowness that sings for all time. Her phrasing is grand, broad, generous, like a rosined bow being pulled across taut strings. As Wagner's Kundry and Fricka, as Strauss's Octavian or Composer, to name just a few of her celebrated gallery of roles, she occupies the music, her whole body the vibrating mechanism of sound—like the wooden structure of the low string instrument.

Christa Ludwig was born into music. Her Viennese father, Anton Ludwig (first a bass, then a baritone, finally a tenor), ran an opera school in Aachen, where the family had moved from Berlin. Her mother, Eugenie Besalla, sang under Herbert von Karajan in Aachen during the 1940s and eventually became her daughter's teacher. Besalla had ruined her voice by singing the wrong roles, by moving up from her natural mezzo tessitura into demanding soprano parts, and she was forced to give up her career at forty. Interestingly, Christa Ludwig too passed through an identical phase of attempting to move up the scale in her repertory, taking on Leonore in *Fidelio*, Ariadne in *Ariadne auf Naxos*, the Dyer's Wife in *Die Frau ohne Schatten*, the Marschallin in *Der Rosenkavalier*, and Lady Macbeth—and forever tempted by the lure of Isolde and Brünnhilde, until better sense ruled under the influence of her mother and the legendary Zinka Milanov.

She was exposed to the stage from the age of three, insisting that as far back as she can remember she knew her mother's roles of Azucena and Ulrica by heart. At eighteen, she made her professional debut in Frankfurt for 400 marks and a pound of coffee. It was just after World War II—and the opera Johann Strauss's *Die Fledermaus*, in which she sang the travesti role of Prince Orlofsky. After five years there, during which time she sang all kinds of roles, Ludwig moved on to Darmstadt with a repertory including Octavian, Ulrica, the Composer in *Ariadne*, Dorabella in *Così fan Tutte*, Carmen, and roles in two operas by

Arthur Honegger. In 1954 she moved on to Hanover and Hamburg, climbing up the ladder in the structure of the German theaters, adding the Princess Eboli in *Don Carlo*, Amneris in *Aida*, and Marie in *Wozzeck* to her credits. And a year later came her Salzburg Festival debut. She was mixing the trouser parts—Cherubino in *Figaro*, Octavian, Composer, Hansel—with such wide-ranging repertory as Brangäne in *Tristan und Isolde*, Ortrud in *Lohengrin*, Kundry in *Parsifal*, and Rosina in *Il Barbiere di Siviglia*, as well as Carmen. The 1959–60 season brought her to America as Dorabella at the Chicago Lyric and to the Metropolitan with Cherubino, Octavian, Amneris, and Brangäne. Later would come more remarkable mixtures, including Waltraute in *Götterdämmerung*, Charlotte in *Werther*, Lady Macbeth, and Klytämnestra in *Elektra*.

After years on the opera stage Ludwig began to confine herself more to lieder and concert appearances, singing her roles primarily at the Vienna State Opera, her home theater since 1955. She had divided her activities fifty-fifty between opera and concerts for years, but after all the stress and strain—and routine—of the stage, she began to weigh her singing toward concerts. Her associations have included Karl Böhm, Herbert von Karajan, and Leonard Bernstein, with whom she has worked extensively. The legendary Walter Legge launched her recording career, often pairing her with his celebrated wife, Elisabeth Schwarzkopf. As Ludwig later reflected, "He taught me how to make the word *sun* shine and how to make the word *flower* bloom." She credits him with forming and changing her way of life, shaping her artistically. "Through him," she has said, "I learned to know what hard work meant, to improve the sound of my voice, to interpret." It was Böhm who discovered her in Hanover and engaged her for Vienna, and their historic collaborations spanned Salzburg to New York.

Onstage Christa Ludwig exudes a certain air of glamour with an earthiness and directness, a complete lack of the superficial or mannered. Her voice springs from the heart of Central Europe, a primordial force that speaks deeply, richly, profoundly in the most human way possible. She is the Earth-Mother of singers.

Kiri Te Kanawa

Just when one feels that the great art of singing and all its glorious tradition are on the wane comes someone to hold back the dusk, the *Götterdämmerung*. New Zealand–born Kiri Te Kanawa is one of these, a precious commodity. Her vocal schooling, her impeccable musicianship, her ravishing physical beauty light up the opera world. She is an unmistakable artist, one who has worked hard and long to master her God-given instrument, who hasn't relied on physical allure alone—although it hasn't hurt either in the women she portrays onstage. Te Kanawa is a proud beauty, darkly sensual, elegant, tall. And the voice has cream in its timbre, spanning the full soprano range with an extraordinary ease and wealth of coloration, expertly developed throughout the full range, flexible, warm, and womanly.

The Countess in Mozart's *Le Nozze di Figaro* revealed her to Britain at Covent Garden and to America at Santa Fe. From then on, she emerged an international figure. Her New York debut in 1974 came about at the eleventh hour at the Metropolitan. She had arrived to sing Desdemona in Verdi's *Otello* at later performances in the run, but at 11 A.M. the day of a national matinee broadcast of the opera, Teresa Stratas became ill, and Te Kanawa went on without rehearsal, scoring a public and critical success. Because she refuses to leave home for more than a few weeks at a time, her opera activity has tended to center around London, where she is revered—so much so that Prince Charles requested she sing at his marriage to Lady Diana in the summer of 1981. There, at St. Paul's, the soprano was heard around the world via television.

Emulating her distinguished and equally glamorous predecessors, Elisabeth Schwarzkopf and Lisa Della Casa, she has flowered in the repertory of Mozart and Strauss, lending such roles as the Countess, Donna Elvira, Fiordiligi, the Marschallin, Arabella, and others an unmistakable luster and beauty. But she has branched out to Violetta in *La Traviata*, Amelia Boccanegra, Desdemona, and Marguerite in *Faust* as well. She has made numerous recordings, and proved to be a director's and cameraman's dream when she played Donna Elvira in Joseph Losey's controversial film of *Don Giovanni*, conducted by Lorin Maazel. She seemed an avenging angel as she swooped down on Palladio country near Venice, where Losey set his concept. Her Rosalinda in *Die Fledermaus*, charming and naughty, became an international hit when telecast from Covent Garden, and television's doors have opened in mini-series and specials designed around her in London.

Te Kanawa is from Gisborne, New Zealand, descended from "ordinary people." Her father is of ancient Maori heritage, her mother Irish with lineage going back to Sir Arthur Sullivan. Her parents decided she should be a singer, and when she was fifteen the family moved from the small town to Auckland, "and the singer part of me took over." New Zealand backed her, and the government financed the young artist to go overseas and study in England. Prizes soon followed. "I always wanted to sing, but I was brainwashed from the age of three. My parents told me, 'You are going to be an opera singer.' My mother played the piano, which I learned first. At eighteen they forced me to decide whether to do it seriously or not, and I said, 'Yes, anything!' I did *not* want to be a shorthand typist."

In 1966 she arrived in England for more studies with Vera Rosza, whom she calls "a milestone in my life, along with my husband." Mme. Rosza, with whom Kiri still works hard and tirelessly, is affectionately known as "the dragon." In her early years, however, Te Kanawa was singing as a mezzo, but the conductor Richard Bonynge told her she was a soprano when he heard her at the London Opera Centre master class. As a student at the Centre, which is attached to Covent Garden, she acquired an agent and auditioned six or seven times for Colin Davis and Peter Hall, who kept asking her to learn this and that. She went on expanding her knowledge of opera, her skills as singer-actress. Then in December 1971 came the big break. Having sung in many Centre productions, with the Northern Opera and New Zealand Opera, in concerts and even at Covent Garden in smaller parts, she assumed the role of the Countess in a new production of *Le Nozze di Figaro* led by Davis, and suddenly she found herself in the international limelight.

Te Kanawa too has become wise, spacing out her performances sensibly and confining the bulk of her work to England. She keeps her vocal technique polished, forever striving to be a more effective singing actress. She's quick and bright, she's a mite impatient and ambitious. But there is an overriding sense of knowing exactly what she wants to do and how she wants to do it. There was a time she did not like to work and had little discipline in her life and career. Today she takes her position seriously and relishes it. Kiri Te Kanawa is the prototypical modern diva.

Gwyneth Jones

From modest beginnings as a lyric mezzo-soprano, the Welsh-born Gwyneth Jones has evolved into a reigning dramatic soprano of her day, her performance schedule crowded with Brünnhilde in the *Ring* cycle, Isolde, Salome, Leonore in *Fidelio*, Senta in *Der Fliegende Holländer*, Ariadne in *Ariadne auf Naxos*, the Marschallin in *Der Rosenkavalier*, Tosca, and many more. Just as Birgit Nilsson began to consolidate her roles and sing less on the international circuit, Miss Jones ascended in a similar repertory. Like many prominent British singers, she comes from Wales, born in Pontwynydd, where she first studied. Between 1956 and 1960 she was a student at the Royal College of Music in London and then at Herbert Graf's International Opera Studio in Zurich, where she began to sing small roles as a mezzo. Shortly thereafter, she switched into the soprano region because the natural placement of her voice had been moving upward. Her first soprano role was Amelia in *Un Ballo in Maschera*, and while in Zurich she had auditioned for and won membership in Covent Garden for the 1963–64 season—but as a mezzo, since that was the kind of voice needed at the time. She sang small roles that first year, but the next she was promoted to Santuzza and covered for Régine Crespin as the *Fidelio* Leonore and for Leontyne Price as the *Trovatore* Leonora, actually filling in for both of them. International recognition followed shortly, and her repertory expanded rapidly and with impressive range, especially in the Italian and German lirico spinto staples: Aida, Elisabetta in *Don Carlo*, Tosca, Madama Butterfly, Senta, Elisabeth, Salome, and eventually the Dyer's Wife in *Die Frau ohne Schatten*. She was singing Verdi and Puccini at La Scala, Strauss in Munich and Vienna, Wagner at Bayreuth while keeping regular seasons at Covent Garden. At the Wagner festival Miss Jones has been in residence for over a dozen years, singing the gamut of Wagner heroines, Senta, Sieglinde, Elisabeth, Kundry, and the three Brünnhildes among them.

In the fall of 1981 she turned to Isolde for the first time, although offers had been made back in the early 1970s. She finds Isolde the dream role of her career, for which everything she had done prepared her. One of the landmarks of her singing life has been the *Ring* as produced at Bayreuth by Patrice Chéreau in 1976 (the centennial of Bayreuth) and which played for four summers, finally recorded and filmed for television before it was retired. She deems it "tremendous, dramatic theater."

Landmark after landmark have built an action-packed career, one that has encompassed a couple of vocal crises as well, but Gwyneth Jones has ploughed right ahead, undaunted. Celebrated for her passionate, all-stops-out interpretations, she projects a wild excitement, sometimes at the expense of vocal purity or steadiness. She says it is a matter of believing in the situation, what is happening. "I study a role, the surroundings, how the characters walk and talk until I find the essence of how they behave. When I make my entrance, it is as if it is happening for the first time. I feel that we all have in us, very often hidden, so many emotions and so many feelings that need to come out. I am always completely immersed in the role. I believe in it completely. But at the same time, you have to control yourself. I am not just wildly emotional. Obviously, one has to learn movement, deportment, facial control, vocal control. It is a two-sided thing, in that you must be able to control every muscle, yet the most important thing is that it come from the heart. Dramatic intensity comes out of me like waves of power, and I feel as if I am sending sparks flying." Summing up her expansive, all-out attitude, she says, "Opera is why I am here—to bring joy to the public. I think of the public as my friends, and I feel I have been given a voice to use the best I can, to bring joy, to lift them into another sphere."

Janet Baker

Dame Janet Baker said farewell to opera during the 1981–82 season—a grand trilogy of Gluck's Alceste at London's Royal Opera House, Donizetti's Maria Stuarda at the English National Opera, and, finally, Gluck's Orfeo at the Glyndebourne Festival. As with everything Dame Janet has done, it was just right. She had reserved her opera activity to the British Isles so she could be close to home during the long rehearsal and performance periods, channeling her energies for the work at hand. And these roles too proved ideal: the classical nobility, both female and male, of her Gluck portrayals, and the tragic, noble Scottish Queen who dies at the hand of Elizabeth I. England has had its brief but illustrious chapter of Dame Janet onstage: Penelope in Monteverdi's *Il Ritorno d'Ulisse* and Cavalli's *Calisto* at Glyndebourne, Octavian in *Der Rosenkavalier* with the Scottish Opera, Dido in Berlioz's *Les Troyens* in Scotland and at Covent Garden, Mozart's *La Clemenza di Tito* in London, and a raft of Handel roles in concert and onstage, including *Giulio Cesare* with the ENO. All were chosen like a fine pair of exact-fitting gloves, bringing out the best of her voice and personality.

For the rest of the world, through concerts and recordings, Dame Janet is a singer of songs—one of enormous skill, penetration, intelligence, concentration, communication. Her recitals over the years tended to become solemn rites, ecstatically received. One felt, as with only a handful of other singers in our time, at the very source with Dame Janet. She takes it all in her stride, and sometimes those vociferous ovations almost seem to embarrass her. She prefers getting down to work and singing. Dame Janet is a realist, a no-nonsense, earnest, honest type. She says she was born with a musician's instinct, a standard for the best. A native of York, she calls her musical background "sketchy." Eventually, the family bought a piano, and she began to play. She first sang as a soprano in the school choir, but when her voice changed she found herself a mezzo—with not only strength and weight in the lower regions but also a remarkable upper extension that has allowed forays into certain soprano repertory. She went to Leeds in Yorkshire to study, toiling as a bank clerk to pay for lessons. From there she went to London, working in a bank by day and traveling in her off-hours to Hampstead for lessons. She was taught from the start that singing must be an easy, natural function, unhampered by any superfluity. Eventually she won the *Daily Mail* Kathleen Ferrier Prize, thereby forming a link to the great English mezzo who tragically died so young. Soon she was singing at Glyndebourne, Aldeburgh, Sadler's Wells, the Scottish Opera, and with the English Opera Group in Purcell, Handel, Mozart, and Britten. Among the singers Dame Janet idolized were Isobel Baillie, Ferrier, and Victoria de los Angeles, whom she calls "a breath of fresh air."

When Janet Baker first emerged on the American scene in 1966, she was thought of primarily as a concert singer and recitalist. It's only in the intervening years that Baker the opera singer has come to the fore. She says she began as a contralto in the repertory works, then as a mezzo in *Dido and Aeneas* and the Handel pieces. She then began to feel the real part of her instrument: "As a mezzo I began using the best part of my voice and a wide range. It was here all the time, it had been trained." Then came that important moment when a singer's technical problems become a thing of the past and she is able to concentrate on interpretation. As Dame Janet has said, the interpretive problems come from the limitations of one's self as a person: "That's the most terrifying thing. We are on a different creative level from the creative process. Composers need us, yes, it's true. But we are on a different plane of existence. Their mission is a higher one. They inspire us—but who inspired them? The greatest thing for us is to make a phrase sound like you never heard it before."

The mezzo believes in her uniqueness, in not imitating another singer. She knows what she can and cannot do, looking at herself vis-à-vis repertory with honesty. Her approach to opera and concerts has been much the same in the process. "Outside things are different, the exteriors of the stage, of lights and costumes and sets and so on. When I act a role onstage...I do as Dido exactly as I do in a great Schubert song. There is a whole opera in *Nuits d'Été*, all compressed into twenty minutes. It's the time factor which alters, not the personal process. I use the same technique, the same acting, the same concentration. I must be just as real in a song as I am as a character." Making it real, making it immediate and to the point, without fuss or excess, are the keys. Dame Janet Baker's art is formidable.

Grace Bumbry

Labels are something Grace Bumbry has never much liked, but she does love creating a stir. The lady has style. Her international career took off in 1961 in the midst of a cause célèbre when she became the first black singer ever to be engaged at the Wagner shrine, the Bayreuth Festival. The twenty-four-year-old mezzo was cast by Wieland Wagner to sing the Venus in *Tannhäuser,* causing a sensation at the sacrosanct Festspielhaus, where she was dubbed *Die schwarze Venus,* a term that immediately filled every magazine and newspaper across Europe.

Bumbry knew all along she was cut out to be larger than life, that she stood out from the crowd of other children. Her father was a freight handler on the cotton-belt railroad, and she describes the family's existence as being "on the wrong side of the tracks, but a *better* neighborhood." Singing in the church choir led her to first prize in a radio contest and eventually to Arthur Godfrey's "Talent Scouts," where she blazed in "O don fatale."

The young artist went on to study in her native St. Louis, Boston, and Chicago, where, at Northwestern University, she met the legendary Lotte Lehmann, who invited her to attend her

master classes at the Music Academy of the West in Santa Barbara. Her mentor then took her off to Europe, where, following a 1960 debut in Paris as Amneris in *Aida*, she signed with the Basel Opera in Switzerland, there to learn repertory and gain stage experience. After Bayreuth, the whole opera world opened up to her. At the Metropolitan Opera, she made her debut as Eboli in *Don Carlo*, fearlessly marching onstage in Act I to sing the intricate, difficult Veil Song with an assurance and hauteur that conquered the public. Grace Bumbry had definitely come home, and that mastermind of career-building, the late Sol Hurok, had her in hand.

A few years later she was in the process of transforming herself into a soprano, since her top tones always had possessed strength, vibrancy, and power. With intense work, her voice became brighter, less mellow in quality, the top more secure in the overall tessitura of the soprano range. But from the beginning Miss Bumbry had a voice that encompassed a vast range. From the age of twelve she sang for pleasure, performing whatever she liked. The first aria she learned during vocal studies was "Pace, pace, mio Dio," a soprano vehicle from *La Forza del Destino*. Her voice easily spanned a high C to low G in the contralto basement. Later, when her career was in full swing, certain roles served to reveal soprano potential, particularly Santuzza in *Cavalleria Rusticana* and Lady Macbeth, which soars up to a D-flat in alt at the end of the Sleepwalking Scene. She says her teacher, Armand Tokatyan, was the first one who made her think she might someday become a soprano. They worked on "O don fatale" from *Don Carlo*, which she had learned transposed down and now relearned it in the higher key. He told her he didn't know what voice category she was but to be careful when she sang. And to this day she looks to works that fit her particular voice and dramatic flair, no matter what the category. Her mezzo roles have encompassed the standard Amneris, Eboli, Azucena, Orfeo, Carmen. But the Lady Macbeth breakthrough, particularly at the Salzburg Festival under Karajan, led to Salome, Norma, Tosca, Gioconda, Abigaille in *Nabucco*, Medea, and other challenging parts. Mme. Lehmann had advised her that eventually she would become the *Ring* cycle Brünnhildes and Isolde. As she confessed in the press, she was getting tired of the same things over and over as a mezzo and wanted to portray more interesting women onstage. Soprano envy—that longing to be a true prima donna—played its part too. Now she's convinced that beyond having changed to the soprano repertory, she has mastered it as well with pianissimi full and round in tone, the weight of the voice well distributed, the bridge between registers smooth. Hers is a sound that pulsates with emotional fervor.

Despite an openly theatrical life style, filled with exotic furs, fast and expensive sports cars, and prima donna antics—all the exterior attributes of a show business career—Bumbry is a fine diva who lives on challenge.

Nicolai Ghiaurov

T here is something about the elemental sound of a Slavic bass that plumbs the soul and sets the imaginative juices flowing. That somewhat gritty tone, that deep black timbre, that air of melancholy and bleakness evoke a special world, one often fraught with grief and despair—even diabolical intent. For the Western world, the galvanic Feodor Chaliapin epitomizes the eternal Russian bass, the figure who left a lasting mark on Tsar Boris Godunov and Boito's Mefistofele, Mussorgsky's Prince Ivan Khovansky, and Massenet's Don Quichote, Borodin's Khan Konchak, and Gounod's Méphistophélès, as well as on other larger-than-life figures. Then came Alexander Kipnis and the Bulgarian bass Boris Christoff—and now another Bulgarian, Nicolai Ghiaurov, who has reigned in this special repertory during the past few decades. Ghiaurov stands tall at the heart of the tortured world of basso monarchs and menaces.

In the mid-1950s Ghiaurov was still a voice student, but one who had earned top honors at the Moscow Conservatory. When he won the Prix de Paris it launched a career that moved in quick progression from world opera center to world opera center, beginning in Europe and eventually concentrating on Milan's La Scala, where he has been a constant presence. Acclaimed appearances in Chicago led to his Metropolitan Opera debut as Méphistophélès in *Faust* in 1965, the last season of the old opera house at 39th Street and Broadway. Everywhere Ghiaurov went it was obvious that a striking sound and figure were carrying on a noble tradition.

But Ghiaurov was not always a singer. In his native town of Velimgrad, Bulgaria, he first attracted attention as a fine pianist, violinist, and clarinetist, displaying musical talents that he joined to those of acting, in both school and professional productions. It was after his voice had changed that signs appeared suggesting he might become a singer—by which time he had set his heart on conducting. Ghiaurov continued to pursue the latter even when, with the help of Bulgarian composer Peter Stainov, he received a vocal scholarship to Moscow, where he remained five years. The basso gives performances that draw on all his various experiences, believing his vocal contribution to opera must be at one with the entire musico-dramatic concept. "The part I choose," he has said, "must be histrionically challenging, emotionally gratifying—something in which I can immerse myself."

Ghiaurov does not seem to emulate the broad theatrics of a Chaliapin—at least those described by writers. Instead, he follows a quiet, more modern approach to Boris or King Philip

or Méphistophélès. Natural height and athletic physique permit him to endow his portrayals with a handsome, virile quality. His long association with La Scala, and particularly with conductor Claudio Abbado, as well as that with Salzburg and Herbert von Karajan, has led to richly delineated interpretations of Fiesco in *Simon Boccanegra,* Banquo in *Macbeth*, King Philip in *Don Carlo*, Zaccaria in *Nabucco*. Meanwhile, his Slavic works encompass *Khovanshchina, Eugene Onegin,* and *A Life for the Tsar.* Comparisons to Chaliapin or even Christoff are always inevitable, even though Ghiaurov prefers to avoid them. "I would rather be a little first Ghiaurov than a big second Chaliapin," he said early in his career. However else he may be characterized, Nicolai Ghiaurov is the present-day king of the tragic and demonic world of basses.

Regina Resnik

Veteran of forty years on the stage, Regina Resnik began as a soprano, eventually transformed herself into a mezzo-soprano, and now often serves as director of some of the operatic works with which she has long been identified. The New York artist made her first opera appearance in 1942 as Verdi's Lady Macbeth with the New Opera Company in Manhattan. In November 1982 she is still onstage, as the Old Countess in Tchaikovsky's *Pique Dame* with the San Francisco Opera. After her debut Resnik became part of the fledgling New York City Opera and then, in the 1944–45 season, just as the war was ending, joined the Metropolitan Opera, bowing in *Il Trovatore* as a substitute for an ailing Zinka Milanov. Resnik sang forty roles in the soprano repertory before she shifted to the mezzo domain, there mastering another forty parts, many of which became definitive interpretations—Klytämnestra in *Elektra*, Mistress Quickly in *Falstaff*, the Old Countess in *Pique Dame*.

Back in the 1940s Resnik won the Met's Auditions of the Air, singing arias from *Macbeth,* Gounod's *Queen of Sheba,* and *Ernani.* She next sang for general manager Edward Johnson and his staff at the Met. Bruno Walter said she looked like Fidelio and asked her to sing Leonore's cruel Act I aria, "Abscheulicher." Eight months later, at the age of twenty, she performed the role with him. With youth and drive on her side, Resnik sailed through demanding spinto and dramatic roles, but the time of reckoning came—and for a second career. In the mid-1950s she stopped and asked herself where she was and where she was going. The moment of truth proved difficult; it took courage to give up such appealing roles as Cio-Cio-San, Donna Anna, Tosca, Aida, Sieglinde (which she had sung at Bayreuth), and others. And she wasn't sure what the next step would be. Resnik felt she had always been a mezzo with a range wide enough to tackle the soprano hurdles. After she restudied and rethought her voice, she achieved darker, fuller, deeper singing. Her range never altered, only the basic tonal quality and color. She took a year's leave of absence from the Met in 1954–55 for study and experiment, first learning Amneris in *Aida,* one of many operas in which she was to sing two leading roles. Her second Met debut came in February 1956 as Marina in *Boris Godunov,* and soon followed Carmen, Ulrica, Amneris, Laura, Herodias, and many other mezzo parts she performed in theaters around the globe. For a while the Met tended to keep her as Marzelline in *Le Nozze di Figaro.* Carmen brought her to Covent Garden in 1957 and then to Vienna in 1959. With this new repertory came the revelation of new talents as an actress, especially as all her lower roles called for tremendous theatricality. Even as the Baroness in Barber's *Vanessa,* which she created at its world premiere at the Met, she sang only a few lines, but her intensity won admiration. Her Klytämnestra became the standard for her time—this ravaged, spent, guilty queen of Mycenae, grappling with her crazed daughter Elektra. It was this kind of extravagant character that brought out Miss Resnik's particular flair for the stage. Whatever the emphasis of the production—and she sang the role everywhere—she kept the figure's essence of tragedy. The mezzo has long championed total theater in her work, going back to her experiences with Wieland Wagner at Bayreuth and then Luchino Visconti and Franco Zeffirelli.

In the early 1970s this concentration on and passion for theatrical values led Resnik to the director's chair as part of a natural, inevitable process. She had never thought about directing, but in doing research for *Carmen* in Seville she was seeking insight into local atmosphere. At the time she was making her debut at the Hamburg State Opera, and Intendant Rolf Liebermann asked her if she would appear in Wieland Wagner's production of *Carmen.* Although she had often credited the German director for developing her dramatic awareness, she turned the part down because she couldn't stylize the life of a gypsy into abstraction and surrealism, as Wieland favored. But, she added, when Liebermann decided to discard this production, she would like to stage a new one. Five years passed, and he asked her. She then turned to a well-known expressionist painter, Arbit Blatas, who she felt would bring the right instincts of structure, color, and light into the theater. After this initial outing, they turned to *Elektra* for Venice and Lisbon, *Falstaff* for Warsaw, *Pique Dame* for Vancouver. In the meantime they also married.

From her long, fruitful experience onstage and a bright, penetrating mind that has engaged in creating so many roles, Regina Resnik continues to extend her life in the theater. Like her collaboration with Blatas, her career is made up of colors, textures, drama. She is a survivor, a prime mover, a thinker, a talker. In directing she relies on a rule handed down from Wieland: "Let the music speak for itself, and you as an actor will superimpose yourself on the music, or sometimes against it, to bring out the story line." Even though her own performance style occasionally veered toward the overdone, she learned that stillness, simplicity, when played against the music, can create a terrifying force. From Wieland she came to appreciate that ongoing dialogue between director and performer which results in the fusion of character and singer.

Birgit Nilsson

At this juncture in opera history, Birgit Nilsson looms as a kind of dinosaur, a behemoth in a time of increasingly small-scale talents and tragic shortage of Wagnerian singers. When Nilsson sings, a gleaming sound fills the theater, making the walls reverberate, thrilling in its intensity, power, and brilliance, gaining strength as it soars up to chilling high C's. The *Ring* Brünnhildes and Isolde are now a part of history. Like her Scandinavian predecessor, Kirsten Flagstad, Birgit Nilsson has set her mark on these roles for all time in the theater and on records. For future generations, it will be Nilsson's exacting standard against which all else will have to be measured.

Born in a small Swedish town, Vastra Karup, Nilsson defied her father's wishes by studying at the Stockholm Royal Academy. Unaware of the opera world, she wanted to be a concert or church singer. And when she came to the Royal Opera in Stockholm she began singing whatever roles she was needed in. In fact, nearly all her major parts were first aired in Stockholm; even after she became a world celebrity she used that theater as a testing ground for new roles. Nilsson's early career was strewn with such demanding parts as Lady Macbeth, Venus, Senta, Sieglinde, and the *Siegfried* Brünnhilde. Her mentor became Fritz Busch, who believed in the young soprano when

few others did. He brought her to Glyndebourne to sing Electra in *Idomeneo*, thus opening up Europe for her. Other leading maestros helped the singer in her development: Hans Knappertsbusch, Erich Kleiber, Karl Böhm, and Georg Solti among them. She came to the Wagner shrine, Bayreuth, in 1953 and some years later fell under the spell of Wieland Wagner, one of the most revolutionary directors of our century. He said of Nilsson that she had become famous before she had become great—and it was he who helped her achieve the latter with a new production of *Tristan und Isolde* in the mid-1960s. He had thought that because of her long experience in the role of Isolde he would be unable to change a thing; but after they had worked for a week, Nilsson was transformed. Later came Elektra in Vienna and Wieland's last *Ring* at Bayreuth before his premature death.

Although best known for her definitive interpretations of the great Wagner heroines, Nilsson has had a stunning success as Strauss's Salome, Elektra, and the Dyer's Wife. Rudolf Bing, while General Manager of the Met, was so taken with her performance as the Judean Princess that he felt a planned gala would not be complete without Nilsson on the program singing the final scene from *Salome*. Knowing the soprano's love of humor, he even offered to have his own head served up on the platter. The proposal proved irresistible, and Nilsson joined the lineup of stars. A famous wit, she is reported to have claimed Bing as a dependent and taken a deduction on her United States income tax.

Outspoken about what a singer is asked to endure onstage in this age of the director, Nilsson has railed against darkness, scrims, elevators, rock-strewn abstract sets, and the rest. "You know, people say we have no Wagnerian singers today. But none of the earlier Wagnerians would have put up with such things. Absolutely not!" she once observed. All through the 1960s and '70s it was unthinkable to do a *Ring* or *Tristan* without Nilsson, and she shuttled between the Metropolitan, San Francisco, Chicago, Vienna, Hamburg, La Scala, and other European centers with these roles, the keeper of the flame. She relates how she learned to find a balance between singing and acting, realizing that the singing must come first if she was to endure in her career. Early in the 1950s she had to find a way of singing over a cold and thereupon discovered an ideal that has served her well ever since: head placement combined with the right breath support, something her teachers had not been able to give her. With it came that awesome ease and stainless-steel tone in the top register, opening to her a wide path into the Italian repertory—*Aida, Un Ballo in Maschera, Tosca,* and, unforgettably, *Turandot*. She is savvy about her voice, knowing to avoid too much chest tone and breaks between the registers. Over the years she came to understand and trust her voice by the physical sensations she felt and the sound she heard in the places she sang. Hers is a soprano that has served brilliantly and tirelessly all these years. It is an unforgettable sound, often likened to a great silver trumpet. Birgit Nilsson already belongs to opera's pantheon.

Nicolai Gedda

This great artist has spent thirty years before the public, and almost as long in front of that cruel examiner of voices, the recording studio microphone—the latter making him one of the most recorded tenors in history, with well over fifty complete operas to his credit, not to mention hordes of solo albums offering everything from arias and songs to traditional Russian folk music. Nicolai Gedda has long reigned as the master of style—or indeed styles, since he speaks eight languages with thorough proficiency. In his performances one feels total perfection as Gedda assumes the French idiom or the Russian or the German, or even English, which he sings better than most Americans or Britons. Russian is his as a virtual birthright, since he was born to Swedish-Russian parents in Stockholm in 1925. Certainly, the melancholy, the air of eternal sadness, the gloomy, romantic depression inherent in certain Russian roles—the doomed Lensky in *Eugene Onegin,* for instance—seem an exquisite cry from the soul as Gedda pours forth haunting, sometimes disembodied tones.

Gedda studied with Karl Marin Oehmann, a leading Swedish Wagnerian tenor in Berlin in the 1930s who had worked with such giants of his day as Furtwängler, Walter, and Klemperer. Together with his New York teacher, Paula Novikova, Gedda feels he was naturally endowed with a solid technique, which has kept his singing on such a secure and consistently high plane these many years. Also a gift from the gods is the artist's easy upper register, a well-placed lyric voice that Gedda had to learn to support and fill out. With these attributes, both given and acquired, he spins out a cool, clear line, free of notable vibrato but rendered expressive by a cultivated handling of words and atmosphere. Thanks to the placement and comfort of his high voice, Gedda often astounds with his ability to sustain vocal grace throughout the most relentlessly elevated tessitura.

The singer made his operatic debut at the Stockholm Opera on April 6, 1952, in Adam's *Postillon de Jongjumeau* with its fiendish aria filled with glorious high D's. That same year he was heard by the record producer Walter Legge, who immediately engaged him as Dimitri for a recording of *Boris Godunov* then being prepared in Paris under Issay Donrowen— the first complete *Boris* made for LP outside Russia. The trip to France led to an engagement for a new production of Weber's *Oberon* at the Paris Opera in 1954. Meanwhile, Gedda auditioned for La Scala and was signed in 1953 for *Don Giovanni* and the premiere of Carl Orff's *Trionfo di Afrodite* with Elisabeth Schwarzkopf. After recording *Faust* under André Cluytens and other works under Herbert von Karajan, he was quickly put under contract by Covent Garden and Vienna. Thus, within two years of his debut, the tenor found himself singing in all the important European capitals, as well as at the Aix-en-Provence festival, where he perfected his Mozart style. Legge had been at the heart of most of this flurry surrounding the young performer, promoting his name all across the Continent. Of his mentor Gedda has said: "He was not only a producer but a great musician. He had enormous insight into vocal technique and phrasing.... Everything he told me was constructive...We sat down and worked out every phase, every detail."

Nicolai Gedda came to America in 1957–58, making his debut at the Metropolitan Opera as Gounod's Faust. He soon established himself in a striking variety of roles: Don Ottavio in *Don Giovanni,* Tamino in *Die Zauberflöte,* Hoffmann in *Les Contes d'Hoffmann,* Des Grieux in *Manon,* Don José in *Carmen,* Roméo in *Roméo et Juliette,* Pelléas in Debussy's opera, Lensky in *Eugene Onegin,* Hermann in *Pique Dame,* Nemorino in *L'Elisir d'Amore,* Rodolfo in *La Bohème,* the Duke of Mantua in *Rigoletto,* Riccardo in *Un Ballo in Maschera,* Elvino in *La Sonnambula,* Arrigo in *I Vespri Siciliani,* Kodanka in Menotti's *The Last Savage,* and even Anatol in the 1957 world premiere of Samuel Barber's *Vanessa* with Eleanor Steber. Elsewhere he has been one of the few modern-day tenors to sing Berlioz's *Benvenuto Cellini* and Rossini's *William Tell,* or Bellini's *I Puritani.* His world career has just kept going, uninterrupted by vocal crises, periods of stoppage, or wrong decisions. He continues to maintain a remarkably high level of performance, appearing only when he feels at least 90 percent well. His training and early experience, his years of work under Beecham, Klemperer, Karajan, Solti, Böhm, Krips, Mitropoulos, and others—all have served him well. If Gedda's admirable artistry failed to make him an international superstar, that simply reflects the kind of person the tenor is: serious, musical, even self-effacing. Still, Gedda knows his worth, and he never gives less than his best, always with the air of an aristocrat. The records alone assure him a firm niche in vocal history.

Jennie Tourel

For decades, a Jennie Tourel New York recital was an event. One knew one would hear German lieder, French chansons, Italian canzone, Russian songs, whatever, done with rare authenticity, charm, and expressivity—"a virtuoso with heart and soul to spare," one critic observed. Throughout her long career Tourel was esteemed as the complete singer with a vast history of song at her fingertips, as well as ten languages, taking her from Monteverdi to Hindemith, always with the last word in stylish know-how. Simplicity and dedication reigned as the key words of Tourel's art. "All singers have to be in love with their work," she said more than once. "It must come from inside."

If the Tourel of the recital stage is the one that stays in the mind, it is because the last years of her career were spent exclusively in this milieu. Her love affair with the stage began in her teens. Not long after she had conquered Paris at the Opéra-Comique, as Bizet's Carmen and Thomas's Mignon, she turned to recitals—and with the same dedication, the same fire. As a young student in Paris, she heard the towering Russian basso Feodor Chaliapin, and it proved one of the greatest experiences of her life. She often liked to quote a bit of advice from his autobiography: "My work had as its leitmotif the struggle against the sham glitter that eclipses the inner light, the complexities that kill simplicity, the vulgar externals that diminish true grandeur." Tourel took this to heart in everything she touched.

Another influence was the brilliant Spanish mezzo-soprano Conchita Supervia, whom she heard in recitals, in Rossini operas, as Carmen, and as Lehár's Frasquita. "I never wanted to meet her, but I went to all her performances. In fact, she gave me the idea of recitals, for she was an exciting performer and a fantastic experience for me. I admired Supervia for her charm and beauty as well as for her ability as a showman with all that temperament." As Carmen or Rossini's Rosina, two roles she sang in America and Europe, Tourel reflected that combination of elegance and fire.

The Canadian-born mezzo (of Russian parents) won an audition in Paris and made her debut at the Comique in 1933 as Carmen, after studies with Anna El-Tour, whose name she anagrammatized for her own. "I had the idea of being on the stage, and I hoped for the best," she reminisced shortly before her death in 1973. "After the performance, the executive director called me in and told me it was beautiful—and gave me a two-year contract. 'You started at the top. What would you like to sing next?' I answered Mignon." And so her route was charted. A few seasons with the Chicago Opera eventually brought her to the Metropolitan in 1937 as Mignon and then to the fledgling New

York City Opera in 1944 as Carmen—and eventually a widespread concert career, culminating with her invaluable teaching at the Juilliard School in New York. In 1951 she created the role of Baba the Turk in Stravinsky's *The Rake's Progress* at La Fenice in Venice, the composer conducting.

With her students, as with herself, she insisted on simplicity, even though she knew it was difficult for most people to be simple onstage. "I never learned how to act," she recalled. "I talk, I don't act, and it has always been this way. Since I started I never liked the superficial. I have to act only as I feel, because that's me. In a song I don't do something just to make an effect, but my imagination is very farfetched. When I sing and I have to re-create the music and the words of two people, I feel what they want to say and then add my own feeling for them, still respecting their value of words and notes. The most difficult thing in life," she believed, "is to be simple—simplicity means much more in communicating. I think it is a matter of age and experience—so a performer should not be afraid to grow up, for there are so many good things that come with it. I matured as an artist, but I did not stop my enthusiasm to be involved in everything I do. You must be excited always in all you do—excited in the best sense of the word. You must burn inside yourself to give and share. When I first began singing songs, I understood I had to give my best, which comes from the heart. The audience has a heart. If what I say goes straight to the heart, then we have communication."

And communicate Jennie Tourel did all her life. She always felt she was repaid for her extraordinary dedication to art in having the chance to work with Arturo Toscanini (who brought her to New York in 1942 for a major chapter in her concert career, to sing Berlioz's *Roméo et Juliette* with the New York Philharmonic), Serge Koussevitzky, Leopold Stokowski, and then Leonard Bernstein, whose First and Third Symphonies she introduced, and with whom she shared a long and fruitful artistic collaboration in countless concerts and recitals. She won the admiration of the toughest critics, Virgil Thomson among them. After her first New York recital in 1943 he wrote in the *Herald Tribune:* "One had the impression of being present at the take-off of some new and powerful airplane for a round-the-world flight.... Miss Tourel is, I believe, unequaled among living singers for the concentration in one artist of vocal skill, sound musicianship and stylistic flexibility." Some thirty years later she was still being admired for these same rare attributes. She pursued the idea that "the road to perfection is as intangible as the road to the stars...the stars are always far away, no matter how high you reach." Jennie Tourel kept reaching.

The
Conductors

Herbert
von Karajan

Glorious orchestral sounds and seamless interpretations constitute the hallmark of the music made by Herbert von Karajan, an artist who stands as the great perfectionist of his age. He is the aloof aristocrat of today's conductors. His devotion to the Berlin Philharmonic and the Salzburg Festival has made him the kingpin of European conductors. He rules with absolute authority, assembling ideal casts, conducting and directing, documenting on records and television. He has the power to hypnotize—those with whom he collaborates and his audience. His performances have a sacred quality about them, as if one were in church receiving the ultimate word. And Karajan revels in his power. Those who work with him seem ready to sacrifice body and soul to his command.

Karajan made his debut in opera in 1929, conducting *Le Nozze di Figaro* in Ulm, a provincial theater. A few years later while he was conducting music for Max Reinhardt's production of Goethe's *Faust* at Salzburg, he learned what undisputed authority was all about, and he discovered that a singular vision of musical and stage performance can be accomplished only when they are in the hands of one person. He moved on to Aachen, where he became Kapellmeister, the youngest Generalmusikdirektor in Germany. Then Heinz Tietjen needed a conductor at the Berlin Opera. Karajan came, thus beginning the long feud with Wilhelm Furtwängler, then head of the Berlin Philharmonic. His admiration of Victor De Sabata led to a long association with La Scala in Milan. Karajan was living in Vienna in the immediate postwar period when his recording career was

launched with EMI, thanks to the efforts and interests the conductor shared with producer Walter Legge. And his worldwide reputation had its genesis in the vast output of records he has made, beginning with the Vienna Philharmonic and the Philharmonia Orchestra of London. Eventually, after 1954, his power extended to running the Vienna State Opera, then the Berlin Philharmonic and Salzburg Festival—the cream of European musical life. Everything Karajan undertakes becomes an event. He eschews racing hither and yon for engagements. His infrequent guest engagements, his tours with the Berlin orchestra or La Scala are made under the most auspicious circumstances.

With his orchestra Karajan explores sound—highly polished, brilliant, razor-sharp in attack, glowing in tone but never thick, always transparent. His concepts stem from the very act of breathing, of forming phrases as he breathes with his players and singers. Like all great maestros, he concentrates on the text, the clarity, and underneath his orchestra plays with that soft cushion of tone that supports the vocal sounds and lets the words emerge, all in a delicate, perfect equilibrium. Karajan insists his players not only listen to one another but to the stage as well, and in this way too he accomplishes an exceptional balance of elements. There is an eternity of line in his readings, as one phrase elegantly dovetails with the next, creating a continuous, faultless fabric. Dramatic power and refinement confront one another in his work, as well as a depth of tone and meaning.

Berlin provided Karajan with a contract for life and the power of absolute authority—a testament to his predecessors von Bülow, Richard Strauss, Mahler, Nikisch, and Furtwängler. At the same time came the opportunity to take over the Vienna State Opera after Karl Böhm's brief tenure, and again Karajan worked wonders, bringing the Staatsoper to the fore as one of the world's reigning houses. By 1964 he was gone, a victim of the ever-current gossip, political tactics, and problems that come with the territory of Vienna. He had first conducted at Salzburg in 1948, but through Furtwängler's double-dealing, he spent seven years away from Mozart's hometown, during which he had a short stay at the postwar Bayreuth Festival. In 1956 Karajan was appointed artistic "leader" of Salzburg, and in 1957 he returned to conduct and produce *Fidelio* and his own *Falstaff,* which had originated at La Scala. Since then he has ruled supreme at Salzburg, conducting and directing a vast span of works, attracting the world's leading singers into his sphere.

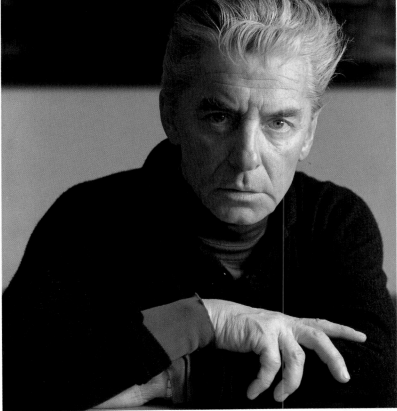

Over the years Karajan has become more and more sparing of movement and gesture in his conducting. The work is accomplished during rehearsals. He seeks to delve into the spirit of the work, of the composer, immersing himself in it and drawing everyone into the work at hand. His ear is extraordinary. He attends to nuance, balance, details, precision in the manner of a fanatic. One feels a superhuman mind at work, one dealing with thousands of details at once, yet never losing the overall picture of any piece of music. There is no showiness in Karajan's work. He just becomes the music in communicating its very essence. Karajan is music's commander in chief.

Erich Leinsdorf

The steel-trap mind of Erich Leinsdorf has made him the storehouse of music and the world that surrounds it, accumulated throughout long years of hard work and fascinating experiences. His opportunities have been vast and varied, a constant interplay of opera and symphonic work that makes up the rich pattern of his career, which includes working with Arturo Toscanini in Salzburg in the 1930s, a long association with the Metropolitan Opera, a stint as music director of the Boston Symphony, and now free-lancing all over the globe.

Born in Vienna, Leinsdorf studied piano with Paul Emerich and composition with Paul Pisk, who came out of the school of Franz Schreker and Arnold Schoenberg. In his native city he heard concerts led by Furtwängler, Kleiber, Klemperer, and Bruno Walter, as well as performances at the Vienna State Opera under the expert guidance of Clemens Krauss. At the Salzburg Mozarteum, the young Leinsdorf worked with Mozart expert Bernhard Paumgartner, and in 1931 he became the coach of tenor Gotthelf Pistor, teaching him Schoenberg's *Gurrelieder* in Vienna and then traveling with the singer to Bayreuth, where he heard Toscanini and Furtwängler at the Wagner shrine. Thanks to his mastery of the Italian language, Leinsdorf began coaching Maria Müller, Luise Helletsgruber, and other members of the Vienna State Opera in the Italian repertory. For the same reason he undertook to coach at Salzburg for a Walter-led production of *Don Giovanni*, aiding the German members of the cast—Lotte Schoene, Helletsgruber, and Emanuel List—who were joining the Italian wing composed of Ezio Pinza, Dusolina Giannini, Dino Borgioli, and Mariano Stabile. There he met Toscanini, who would have the most profound influence on the budding conductor, and whose assistant Leinsdorf became in 1935 for Salzburg performances of *Fidelio* (with Lotte Lehmann) and *Falstaff.* Toscanini had forged a strong bond with the aging Verdi, and so Leinsdorf experienced the late Verdian style almost first-hand. That same year he had assisted Walter with *Die Entführung aus dem Serail* for the Maggio Musicale Fiorentino. In 1936 he returned to Salzburg to prepare *Die Meistersinger* with Maria Reining, Charles Kullmann, and Hans Herman Nissen, a significant occasion since it marked Toscanini's leading Wagner outside Bayreuth. After the Italian maestro had moved *Fidelio* intact to Vienna, young Leinsdorf went on to Italy for short seasons there, doing *Meistersinger* in Bologna and *Arabella* and *Parsifal* in Trieste, all arranged by Toscanini.

In 1937 Leinsdorf was again at Salzburg with Toscanini, this time for *Die Zauberflöte,* and in November of that year he received an offer to come to the Metropolitan Opera as part of manager Edward Johnson's plan to relieve the overworked Artur Bodanzky, who had long been in charge of the German wing. At age twenty-five, Leinsdorf made his debut on January 21, 1938, with *Die Walküre,* after only a few days' notice—and in the realm of the giants, since the cast included Kirsten Flagstad, Elisabeth Rethberg, Paul Althouse, Ludwig Hofmann, and Emanuel List, truly the cream of contemporary Wagnerians. In quick succession he moved on to *Elektra, Lohengrin, Tannhäuser,* and *Parsifal,* ending with a two-year contract. Although terribly short on experience, he had leapt into the international spotlight, but as always, before or since, Leinsdorf was faultlessly prepared. In 1938 he bowed at the San Francisco Opera, then directed by Gaetano Merola. Back at the Met, he conducted *Pelléas et Mélisande* and assisted Fritz Reiner with *Elektra* and *Meistersinger.* In 1939 he led *Fidelio* with Flagstad, Melchior, and Kipnis.

In 1943, with these years of total concentration on opera behind him, Leinsdorf became head of the Cleveland Orchestra, replacing Artur Rodzinski, who was moving on to the New York Philharmonic. He stayed three years, before going to the Rochester Philharmonic in 1947, where he remained nine years. Just after the war, he had returned to his native Vienna to lead *Fidelio* and Weinberger's *Schwanda,* only to depart again, this time for twenty-six years. During a single disastrous season, he took charge of the New York City Opera, producing the local premieres of Orff's *Der Mond,* Martin's *The Tempest,* and Floyd's *Susanna,* as well as Offenbach's *Orpheus in the Underworld.* Meanwhile, Rudolf Bing had come to New York in 1950 as general manager of the Metropolitan Opera, and in 1957 he invited Leinsdorf to return to the house for the American premiere of Strauss's *Arabella* with Eleanor Steber, Hilde Gueden, Blanche Thebom, and George London. It proved a triumph for all concerned. And that same year Bing asked the conductor to become part of the management now that Max Rudolf was about to take over the Cincinnati Symphony. For the next five years Leinsdorf served as musical consultant to the Met, a house that he always refers to as his "second home" in the United States. During this period he also began a long association with RCA Victor, for which he made a dozen and a half complete operas.

Leinsdorf once again changed courses when in 1962 he took the reins of the Boston Symphony upon the retirement of Charles Munch, staying there seven years, during which time he brought innovative programming and a new profile to the orchestra. At the summer Tanglewood Festival he performed several operas with the Boston Symphony, among them *Zauberflöte,* the first version of *Fidelio, Entführung aus dem Serail, Lohengrin,* and *Otello.* Since that time Leinsdorf has pursued a highly successful free-lance career, while maintaining his old ties with the Met, where he continues to lead performances of Wagner, Strauss, Mozart, and Verdi. For Bayreuth he did *Tannhäuser* in 1971, and he has also appeared at the Teatro Colón in Buenos Aires. In 1970 he helped inaugurate the new theater of the Juilliard School at Lincoln Center with a performance of Stravinsky's *The Rake's Progress.*

Leinsdorf's conducting evinces a finely honed mind at work. In everything he does the maestro supplies a vast, detailed blueprint of the intentions stated in the score. With absolute musical accuracy, he approaches each piece in a superbly analytical manner. Always devoted to the pursuit of style, Leinsdorf has never failed to master not only a particular piece of music but also the complete works of a composer and even the milieu in which he wrote. The conductor's performances are known less for their blazing passion than for their "interpretive" quality. They reflect a streamlined, clear-eyed overview of the music, led with a brisk efficiency, a tight hand, and an intellect that has absorbed and digested a fund of knowledge and wisdom. Leinsdorf is the kind of conductor no age should be without.

Karl Böhm

Roars of approval greeted his every arrival in the pit and then onstage during the final bows, confirming that Karl Böhm was the grand old man of music, a superb, eloquent artist whose illustrious career had long since endowed him with a legendary halo. And how he relished it! When the maestro died in Salzburg on the eve of his eighty-seventh birthday in August 1981, he had received every honor possible in his native country. Unlike so many conductors, Böhm knew and loved the human voice, and he knew who was capable of what. He worked with and cultivated the cream of many decades, from Maria Reining and Maria Cebotari in the prewar years to Leonie Rysanek, Birgit Nilsson, Christa Ludwig, Agnes Baltsa, and Edita Gruberova at a later time, all documented on so many definitive recordings. Böhm's performances in America and Europe bore the stamp of a major event, and the vintage quality of his readings made audiences feel they had drunk at the source. Under his hand, a major orchestra playing the music of Richard Strauss sounded as it did under no one else. Böhm's career spanned a good part of this century; filled with distinction, it contributed mightily to the ongoing tradition of music.

Karl Böhm was born in Graz in the Styrian sector of Austria, his family German-Bohemian on one side and French-Alsatian on the other. The elder Böhm insisted that Karl follow in his footsteps, which meant earning a doctorate in law. Still, having already mastered piano and violin, the young man nurtured his inclination to music with studies in the strict Vienna school of Eusebius Mandyczewski, with whom he learned harmony, counterpoint, and composition. As for becoming a conductor, Böhm was wont to quote Hans Richter who once said to the aspiring musician: "Simply so: one mounts the podium, and either one knows how to conduct or one will never learn it!" Eventually, Böhm became coach and assistant conductor in the opera house at Graz, rehearsing incidental music for plays. In compensation for this enormous workload, he was awarded his first opera in October 1917, Viktor Nessler's *Trompeter von Sakkingen.* In 1919 the newly graduated Doctor of Law led *Der Fliegende Holländer.* Böhm's father was an amateur singer and Wagner enthusiast, making pilgrimages to Bayreuth and befriending Wagner singers and conductors, most notably Hans Richter. Although influenced by this example, Böhm felt he achieved real insight into Wagner's music only through Karl Muck, considered the finest *Parsifal* conductor of his generation. Muck and Richard Strauss became his models. After hearing Böhm lead a performance of *Lohengrin,* Muck offered to study all the Wagner scores with the fledgling conductor. But it was Beethoven's only opera, *Fidelio,* that became what Böhm called his "song of destiny," a work that he led first in 1920–21 for the composer's 150th birthday and then again that historic night in November 1955 when the mighty paean to human liberty served to open the renovated Vienna State Opera.

During his long career, Böhm conducted some 160 operas, a repertory that stressed Mozart, Wagner, and Strauss, even as the maestro insisted that he loved all good music, including the creations of twentieth-century modernism. At

Darmstadt he produced Krenek's *Jonny Spielt Auf* and *Das Leben des Orest*, Hindemith's *Neues vom Tage*, Honegger's *Judith*, Wolf-Ferrari's *Sly*, and Berg's *Wozzeck*, which he championed worldwide and whose composer became a lifelong friend. Later he would premiere *Lulu* in Vienna and lead the first Paris, Italian, Buenos Aires, and Metropolitan Opera stagings of *Wozzeck*. At the Met too Böhm conducted house premieres of Strauss's *Ariadne auf Naxos* and *Die Frau ohne Schatten*, both extraordinary hits with the public.

Before going to Darmstadt, Böhm accepted an invitation from Bruno Walter to become fourth conductor of the Bavarian Opera House in Munich. There, after trial performances of *Der Freischütz* and *Madama Butterfly*, he was accepted as a full conductor, eventually leading 528 performances of 73 operas, first under Walter's management and then under that of Hans Knappertsbusch, who became music director in 1922. During his Munich period Böhm led his first Mozart opera (*Die Entführung aus dem Serail*), his first *Tristan und Isolde*, and his debut performances of Strauss's *Der Rosenkavalier* and *Ariadne*, the latter his favorite in the Strauss canon. In 1927 he went to Darmstadt with a six-year contract, offered by Carl Ebert, who had the young Rudolf Bing as his administrative assistant. Then Leopold Sachse, general manager of the Hamburg State Opera, brought Böhm to the Hanseatic port, and it was there that the conductor made personal contact with Strauss, when the latter asked his advice on effecting some cuts in *Arabella*. Later Böhm would refer to himself as the "counselor on earth" for Strauss. When pressured to join the Nazi party in order to secure his future in Hamburg, he declared: "I belong to one party only: Music." Böhm never became general manager in the north, but he was soon invited for a guest appearance in Dresden, where Fritz Busch had been forced to relinquish his position a few months earlier. In Dresden Böhm had access to the superb Saxon State Orchestra and a roster of outstanding singers.

In 1938 Böhm made his initial appearance at the Salzburg Festival, where he took charge of a *Don Giovanni* starring Ezio Pinza, Elisabeth Rethberg, Cebotari, and Anton Dermota. Thereafter he returned every summer, and his Mozart-Strauss performances became legendary, particularly *Così Fan Tutte*, first with Irmgard Seefried, Schöffler, Dermota, and Frich Kunz, later with Elisabeth Schwarzkopf, Christa Ludwig, Graziella Sciutti, Hermann Prey, and Karl Dönch. In postwar Vienna Böhm helped create a celebrated Mozart style, together with Josef Krips, performing in the Redoutensaal of the Imperial Palace. Later came profound associations with the Bayreuth Festival and Wieland Wagner for an historic *Tristan* and *Ring* cycle, and then his tenure in New York with the Metropolitan, beginning in 1957 with a new production of *Don Giovanni*, designed by Eugene Berman and sung by Eleanor Steber, Lisa Della Casa, Cesare Siepi, Cesare Valletti, and Fernando Corena. Böhm attributed his lifelong love of Mozart to Strauss, whom he found the ideal Mozart conductor. Of his relationship with the Vienna Philharmonic, the Berlin Philharmonic, and other reigning orchestras, he once declared: "Perhaps they love to make music with me because I am the musicians' friend. Yes,

during rehearsals a conductor has to be pedantic in order to gain respect, but at performances he should be confident enough to give his musicians some freedom within the framework of his concept. And once a Mozart opera has started, the singers have to feel absolutely sure of themselves, independent of any cues from the conductor."

Böhm's conducting stressed a sound that was soft, round, filled with inner life, combining Apollonian and Dionysic virtues. He has said: "I learned a thing or two from Strauss. He conducted with the greatest ease. But, believe me, it's not enough to know an orchestra and many works. The meaning of the music has to be understood and felt, and this requires self-discipline and the gift for teaching discipline to others. Again and again, one is challenged to do one's very best, and even if all true artists always strive to do their best, the best just cannot be produced on the assembly line."

Vienna and Böhm will be forever united, for the maestro became music director of the State Opera in 1943, only to have his post terminated two years later when the Opera House was mistakenly bombed by the United States Air Force. After the war he conducted performances at the interim Theater an der Wien, and when the big house reopened in 1955 he was Operndirektor. But as often happens, things went wrong politically, and he had left by August 31, 1956, replaced by Herbert von Karajan. Meanwhile, his relationship with the Philharmonic remained strong, so that eventually Böhm claimed its Ring of Honor, became an honorary life member, and, in 1967, honorary conductor. In 1964 he was named Austrian Generalmusikdirektor, but what he loved best was being made honorary citizen of Salzburg, for in this way be became a compatriot of Mozart.

It was in Salzburg, at his Schubert House, that Karl Böhm died in 1981. He had just completed his final project that June, a television *Elektra* in which Leonie Rysanek—one of the maestro's beloved singers and a colleague since 1954—sang the title role for the first time in her career. The soprano recalled so many collaborations—*Fidelio* for the centennial of the Vienna State Opera in 1969 and for Beethoven's bicentennial at the Met in 1970; the triumphs of *Die Frau ohne Schatten* in Vienna, New York, Salzburg, Berlin, Paris, San Francisco; the 1965 *Ring* at Bayreuth; and, finally, *Elektra*, after which he collapsed. And so she wrote: "I hardly know of a conductor who loved the human voice as much as he did. He was a feared, strict, unrelenting, unsentimental servant of the score. He hated sentimentality, yet he always evoked genuine feeling, whether in classical, romantic, or contemporary music. He loved applause, the adoration when he took a bow, because it became the triumph of *his* ensemble. In his sparse conducting style, the emotion-filled accents of the music, the crescendos, emerged with a youthful exuberance that always distinguished him, right through his final performance, in spite of noticeable physical weakness. He took his strength from love of the human being—family, friends, artists—and always the music." He had said: "The day I cannot serve music anymore, cannot conduct anymore, I wish to withdraw from this world." Even to the end, Karl Böhm had his way.

James Levine

In talent, in spirit, in sheer energy, in his capacity for work, his optimism, and his response to challenge, James Levine is quite simply prodigious. He seems driven to achieve, to produce, to prove his superhuman versatility, not only as music director and chief conductor of the Metropolitan Opera, but also as a guest conductor on the international circuit, a chamber music performer, an accompanist of and collaborator with singers, and a pianist. At thirty-three he was already music director of the Met, just a few years in the wake of his auspicious debut there with *Tosca* in June 1971. Since then this Wunderkind has managed to leave his imprint on the company with magnetic force, recharting its repertory, gradually building the orchestra into a superb ensemble, developing his own stars and coterie of young artists.

Levine's fascination with opera goes back to his youth in Cincinnati, where established singers remember a chubby little boy who was forever hanging around rehearsals and backstage at the summertime Zoo Opera. As a teenager he commuted to New York every other week to take piano lessons from that doyenne of teachers, Rosina Lhevinne, at the Juilliard School, and he began to frequent the old Metropolitan at Thirty-ninth Street and Broadway. Once a full-time conducting student at Juilliard, Levine attended Met performances and rehearsals several times a week. At the Aspen Festival he became accompanist for the classes of Jennie Tourel, and from her he absorbed a great deal about singing and opera. His conducting teacher Jean Morel and his mentor George Szell, music director of the Cleveland Orchestra, revealed a still broader horizon in the world of opera. After his initial success at the Met, Levine was asked to become principal conductor. Later, with managerial reorganization, he assumed the music directorship, in tandem with stage director John Dexter and chief administrative officer Anthony A. Bliss.

During this period Levine has built an astonishing record of accomplishment, since he often leads nearly half of the season's repertory, ranging from Mozart's *Così Fan Tutte, Don Giovanni,* and *Entführung aus dem Serail* to Berg's *Lulu* (in the full three-act version) and *Wozzeck,* Debussy's *Pelléas et Mélisande,* and a Stravinsky bill of *Le Sacre du Printemps, Le Rossignol,* and *Oedipus Rex.* His basic repertory encompasses the bulk of Verdi— *Luisa Miller, Otello, Rigoletto, Il Trovatore, I Vespri Siciliani, La Forza del Destino, La Traviata, Aida, Don Carlo, Falstaff*—as well as Wagner's *Lohengrin, Der Fliegende Holländer, Tannhäuser,* and *Parsifal* and Puccini's *Tosca, La Bohème, Il Trittico,* and *Manon Lescaut.* Although not a professed Straussian, he has led *Salome, Ariadne auf Naxos, Der Rosenkavalier,* and *Elektra,* while extending his repertory to include *Il Barbiere di Siviglia, Norma, The Bartered Bride, Eugene Onegin, Cavalleria Rusticana, Pagliacci,* and yet more. A regular guest at the Salzburg Festival since 1976, the American conductor has made his mark there with *La Clemenza di Tito, Die Zauberflöte,* and *Les Contes d'Hoffmann.* The summer of 1982 saw his debut at the Bayreuth Festival, where he conducted the centenary performances of *Parsifal.* Meanwhile, Levine maintains his directorship of the Ravinia Festival, the summer home of the Chicago Symphony, there leading concerts, playing chamber music, and accompanying soloists. Between 1974 and 1978 he served as music director of

the Cincinnati May Festival, for which he conducted a variety of choral works as well as Gluck's *Orfeo ed Euridice,* Gershwin's *Porgy and Bess, Lohengrin, Tannhäuser,* and *Parsifal,* all in concert performances.

It is at the Metropolitan, however, that Levine has had the greatest impact, in the sense of a gradual and steady building toward higher and more solid artistic accomplishment. Regular collaboration with the orchestra has resulted in a soaring level of orchestral playing, always with greater homogeneity, richer tone quality, and more symphonic character than the Met ensemble has known in years, or even decades. The continual process of refining certain productions, carried out over several seasons, has yielded performances of extraordinary quality. The choral singing has also improved measurably, so that the powerful scenes of *Tannhäuser, Parsifal, Otello,* or *Oedipus Rex* can be startling in their communication, their massed sound, their brilliance of attack and fullness. And as the musical standard of the house rises, it provides a welcome antidote to the world-wide shortage of big-league voices, those individual singers who, on the terms of a different era, could all by themselves make opera a thrilling experience. Levine's work at the Met may be compared with that of Toscanini during the first years of Giulio Gatti-Casazza's tenure, when the musical criteria at the house attained new heights, impelled there by a major conductor. Thanks to Levine's vision, the Met has broadened its repertory rather considerably, relative to Rudolf Bing's conservative estimate of the subscription audience. Since 1975 Levine has progressively refurbished the standard repertory, mounted a cycle of Mozart operas, explored some neglected works of the past, and produced several masterpieces of twentieth-century opera. Confronted with such strong musical leadership, the once-reactionary public has done an about-face and accepted *Lulu, Wozzeck, Pelléas,* and *Billy Budd,* along with a three-part French evening, *Dialogues des Carmélites,* and the Stravinsky centennial trilogy. For *Parsifal* Levine not only realized one of his own finest readings—miraculously spacious yet forcefully controlled—but also drew from the orchestra one of its most impressive performances, deep in both tone and spirituality. Simultaneously there have been the vigor of his early Verdi and the mature thundering of his *Otello.* To everything he touches Levine brings a sense of pulsating energy and forward drive.

Born in Cincinnati in 1943, James Levine first came to the fore as a piano prodigy, playing the Mendelsohn Second Piano Concerto with the Cincinnati Symphony at the age of ten. He began work in general musicianship with violinist Walter Levin of the La Salle Quartet, a musical relationship that has lasted until today. At the Marlboro School in Vermont he continued work in chamber music but also undertook to assist in a production of *Così Fan Tutte.* At Aspen, Colorado, he studied piano with Rosina Lhevinne, although by that time he had his eye on conducting more than anything else. At the Juilliard School Levine majored in conducting while continuing his studies with Mme. Lhevinne. He became a student of Jean Morel, the French conductor at the Met and the New York City Opera, and when Morel was leading French opera, young Levine sat in on all the rehearsals and with his teacher discussed the fine

points of making music. Altogether, it is the nine consecutive summers at Aspen and the work with Levin and Mme. Lhevinne that shaped the musical personality of the early Levine. Contact at Aspen with Wolfgang Vacano gave him his first chance to conduct opera. Then, in his fourth year at Juilliard, he participated in a Ford Foundation workshop for young conductors at the Peabody Conservatory. One of the instructors was George Szell, who asked Levine to audition for an assistantship with the Cleveland Orchestra, and in 1965 Levine joined that staff, remaining there until Szell's death in 1970.

During this time, and while he was organizing and conducting summer opera at Meadowbrook in Ohio, Levine was exposed to myriad personalities and influences. But he names three seminal inspirations: Toscanini, Callas, and Wieland Wagner. The example of the old maestro taught him to appreciate the value of remaining true to the composer's score and intentions, also what a conductor should be as a force for vitality and truth in music. Callas—her expressivity, her ability to capture the feeling and substance of music, her instinct for communicating what the composer put on paper—struck Levine as the singing counterpart to Toscanini. During trips to Bayreuth, Levine witnessed the theater of Wieland Wagner and the power it exerted on the individual imagination as it interacted with music. The young conductor was impressed with

the controversial manner in which Wieland moved the operatic art form ahead by endowing it with dramatic perception and psychological insight.

Levine's first professional appearances as an opera conductor came with the Welsh National Opera in 1970—*Aida* and *Il Barbiere di Siviglia*—followed by a debut with the San Francisco Opera. It was there, during a performance of *Tosca*, that he caught the eye and ear of a member of the Met administration. By 1971 he was at the Met, leading *Tosca*, which he also conducted for Dorothy Kirsten at Los Angeles' Greek Theater that summer. (As a youngster he had presented himself backstage in Cincinnati to inform the veteran soprano that one day he would conduct *Tosca* for her.)

Observing James Levine, one senses that music lives in him, coursing through his bloodstream. He is a complete, natural musician, for whom making music is a crucial element of life. His music is vivid, dynamic, fluent. He worries about style, about always improving, about artistic growth, about making a genuine creative contribution. He thrives on challenges, on a massive work load. He is organized, goal-oriented, ambitious. Everything he has done or does is a part of a greater plan. With single-minded drive and vision James Levine has forged ahead so that long before reaching the age of forty he had arrived at the very pinnacle of his profession.

Lorin Maazel

Along with many another American musician, Lorin Maazel was a Wunderkind who traveled to Europe to make his name. By the early 1960s he had landed the music directorship of the Deutsche Oper Berlin, and now he holds the full reins of the Vienna State Opera, in the wake of such illustrious predecessors as Gustav Mahler, Richard Strauss, Karl Böhm, and Herbert von Karajan. Meanwhile, at various times, he also headed the Berlin Radio Orchestra, the National Orchestra of Paris, and the Cleveland Orchestra, the latter upon the death of the giant who built it, George Szell. Throughout his career Maazel has journeyed back and forth between a purely symphonic career and one steeped in opera, each nourishing and enriching the other.

Maazel was born in Paris, where his parents had gone to study music. When the family returned to America they settled in Pittsburgh, and there the young Lorin grew up. One day, while watching his son play the piano, the elder Maazel suddenly felt he might have a talent for conducting. And so he tested the child by having him play along with records. Soon Lorin was studying violin with Vladimir Bakaleinikoff, and today he remains a skilled violinist. But his studies went beyond music to embrace philosophy and languages. At the same time, the young Maazel joined the Pittsburgh Symphony's violin section, where he gathered experience in front of rather than on the podium. Later, however, he became assistant conductor. As a prodigy of nine he had conducted at the Interlochen Music Camp and soon after had begun his national career by leading Toscanini's NBC Symphony. In 1952 Maazel went back to Europe on a Fulbright Scholarship to do research on Baroque music in Italy, where in 1953 he led his first European concert, as a last-minute substitute for an ailing conductor. From those provincial beginnings Maazel found his way to La Scala, Bayreuth (the first American and the youngest conductor ever to wield a baton there), Salzburg, and then back to America. The 1962–63 season saw him at the Metropolitan Opera as guest conductor for *Der Rosenkavalier* and *Don Giovanni*.

Responding to the lure of opera, Maazel went to Berlin, where Gustav Rudolf Sellner was the Intendant, in the hope of learning about opera administration and the inherent problems of the opera house. There he became active in choosing repertory, in casting and engaging singers, as well as in overseeing all musical matters. At the time of his arrival in 1965, the Deutsche Oper had a reputation as a tight ensemble (which included a large number of American singers) with a somewhat restricted repertory and a penchant for contemporary opera. Maazel encouraged the latter but insisted on performing the Italian works in the original language, a policy that gradually brought the company into the international sphere. While adding such staples as *La Traviata, Tosca,* and the *Ring* cycle, long absent from the Berlin stage, the conductor engaged a wider array of world-caliber artists for guest appearances, thereby altering the theater's strictly ensemble character. During his tenure the Deutsche Oper gave 270 performances a season with a working repertory of 65 productions, 45 of which were offered in a given season, as many as 15 or 20 led by Maazel. His passion for opera flourished, and he once said: "When I talk about what I love in music, it always ends up a discussion of opera, because I think composers wrote their best music for opera. Mozart certainly did. And the reason composers still do is that they can be uninhibited. Look at the three-bar bridge for Germont's entrance in the second act of *La Traviata,* or the magical sound of the Sailor's voice coming in over the double basses at the end of the *Tristan* prelude. Can there be anything more fantastic?"

With the long siege of opera and the opera house behind him, Maazel decided at age forty that he would retire from it, still refreshed by his work and before the routine could pall. Thus, in 1971 he stepped aside and became music director of the Cleveland Orchestra and chief of the Orchestre National de Paris. Simultaneously, he involved himself in such diverse projects as the controversial Lavelli-Bignens *Pelléas et Mélisande* at the Paris Opera, *Die Entführung aus dem Serail* at the 1980 Salzburg Festival, a film-recording project of *Don Giovanni* (directed by Joseph Losey, with Ruggiero Raimondi and Kiri Te Kanawa, for worldwide distribution), and a cycle of Puccini operas for CBS. He even wrote, produced, and directed a satiricial film about "one week in the life of a conductor" for French television.

And now Vienna, an admittedly dangerous position, thanks to the city's long, notorious history of intrigue, discontent, and sabotage. Maazel thought it over carefully before accepting, but because he and the Austrian government came to the same conclusion—that the same person must be in charge of both artistic and administrative matters, as in Mahler's day—he agreed. He had learned in Berlin that an artistic director without authority over administration can accomplish very little. Maazel relished the thought of conducting less (only some thirty evenings a season) while working creatively on a program likely to have an impact on the whole cultural life of the city, even the world, a program exploiting all the technical means available today: records, film, television.

The product of a clean, clear, linear approach to music, Lorin Maazel's conducting is notable for its transparent voicing, a modern, tensile strength, and a brilliant, almost nervous edge. The style bristles with electricity, even when it fails to exude warmth or lushness. Maazel is a modern, an artist with a highly developed intellect and a quick, razor-sharp mind. Of conducting he has said: "To me making music means to see a certain dimension, a dimension which is also perceived and shared by those who love to listen to music. It is really a spiritual experience and the artist who interprets music must in fact have this sense of the spiritual together with this intellectual perspective, or else he cannot bring out what he wishes to express spiritually." Lorin Maazel is the Man of Reason among today's conductors.

Claudio Abbado

Born to music, Claudio Abbado has reaped the gains of the past to become a leader of the new generation. His father, Michelangelo, is a violinst, composer, musicologist, and author; his brother a pianist and director of the Verdi Conservatory in Milan. Now an internationally acclaimed conductor, Abbado has for years brought the finest musical standards to La Scala, the hub of Italian opera. He reigns there as a home-grown product, having been born in Milan in 1933 and raised in a house bursting with music. At eight he began piano, theory, and harmony, but not until sixteen did he become really serious about music. At that time he entered the Verdi Conservatory to study piano, composition, and conducting, the latter with Antonino Votto, Toscanini's assistant in the early 1920s. At La Scala Abbado heard Toscanini, Furtwängler, Bruno Walter. Later he studied at Salzburg and attended master classes in Siena, after which he went, on his close friend Zubin Mehta's advice, to the master classes of Hans Swarowsky at the Vienna Music Academy. From Swarowsky he learned the value of a finely honed technique, of establishing good eye communication with the orchestra, and the concept of achieving maximum results with the most economical means. In Vienna Abbado heard concerts under Walter and Karajan and became acquainted with the Viennese school of Berg, Schoenberg, and Webern, composers who went unheard in wartime Italy. The aspiring maestro then came to America and the Berkshire Music Center at Tanglewood, where he won the Koussevitzky Prize. In 1958 he made his opera debut at Trieste's Teatro Communale, leading Prokofiev's *Love for Three Oranges*. He taught chamber music for two years at the Conservatory of Parma, where he prepared Hindemith's *Hin und Zurück*. On November 24, 1960, he made his debut at Piccola Scala with a gala concert celebrating the 300th birthday of Alessandro Scarlatti. Abbado returned to the United States to enter the Dimitri Mitropoulos Competition in New York, which he won, thereupon becoming assistant conductor to Leonard Bernstein and the New York Philharmonic for a season. In 1963 he made his Salzburg debut at the invitation of Karajan, and in 1966 he led his first new production at La Scala, Bellini's *I Capuleti e i Montecchi* with Renata Scotto and Giacomo Aragall. In 1968, after his success with Rossini's *Il Barbiere di Siviglia* at Salzburg, the 35-year-old conductor was appointed music director of La Scala. That same season he came to the Metropolitan Opera for *Don Carlo*. In 1971 Abbado was named principal conductor of the Vienna Philharmonic and principal guest of the London Symphony. In 1979 he accepted the directorship of the London Symphony, combining this responsibility with his duties at La Scala.

In the Italian theater Abbado has weathered some turbulent times—financial crises, upper echelon defections, internal politics, and union discord—all mirroring the changing social fabric of Italy itself. But he has managed to broaden the house's activities to include student and worker performances, greater attention to contemporary music, and international tours for the ensemble. Indeed, the Abbado regime demonstrates how a theater must adapt to the world in which it functions. By 1977 the maestro stood as the theater's artistic director, just in time for La Scala's fourteen-month bicentennial celebration, which he launched with a full five-act *Don Carlo* that restored much of the original music, making it the most complete version presented in a major opera house. As a modern musician concerned for his time and place, Abbado doesn't believe that music and music-making can be isolated from society or from the ideologies and events of everyday life. He has said: "Like all human endeavors, music can be utilized for good and bad purposes, and for me the proper utilization of music is as important as its proper interpretation. My duty is not only to give the correct value to

notes or to balance the sonority of an orchestra on the basis of certain criteria or taste. My duty consists of ascertaining that the best performances have the best destination."

Claudio Abbado is a purist, looking to the past to form his own present. He leads all his scores from memory, convinced that if he doesn't know the music by heart, he doesn't know it well enough to conduct. He admires the great maestros of the past, most especially Toscanini, Furtwängler, and Walter, different as they were from one another. Toscanini became an inspiration during those historic and emotional concerts at La Scala immediately after the war, and Furtwängler in 1950 when he led the *Ring* there with Kirsten Flagstad. "Toscanini was for me the greatest conductor," he reflects. "What he was able to achieve from an orchestra, from the singers, was the maximum. On the other hand, Furtwängler was the great musician, the greatest model of a musician for me, especially in the German repertory. And Bruno Walter—his Mozart was magnificent." In Walter's Mozart Abbado finds a unique calm, a tranquility, a musical breathing, a simplicity.

Always the perfectionist, Abbado refuses to perform without proper preparation and insists on lengthy rehearsal periods. He likes to work calmly for extended durations. For him, an opera requires not only many rehearsals but also close collaboration with the set designer, the director, the artists. Scrupulous and serious, he has championed scores that go back to the composer's original intentions—the restored *Don Carlo*, the Zedda editions of *Barbiere* and *Cenerentola*, and the Oeser edition of the original opéra-comique *Carmen*. His readings of *Simon Boccanegra* or *Macbeth*—with their rigorous fidelity to the text and their Herculean sense of drama, of theater—lay bare the elemental Verdi with all the human power and vitality possible. Claudio Abbado is the very model of a modern maestro, but his roots reach far and deep for their sustenance.

Georg Solti

Solti is a Hungarian word that in the 1970s and 80s has stood for sold-out houses, roaring audiences, best-selling, prize-winning records, triumphant tours, excitement possibly unequaled since the turbulent heyday of Toscanini—and a cultish mystique not unlike that surroundng top rock stars. During his tenure with the Chicago Symphony, Georg Solti has managed to set a new standard for the versatile, virtuoso orchestra, and the frenzy stirred by his very presence on the Chicago podium is something to quicken the blood. His concerts become the events of the season—especially when the maestro chooses to do an opera in concert. For all intents and purposes, Solti seems virtually incapable of going wrong, although some might welcome intellectual depth and soul-searching as occasional alternatives to the dynamic physical prowess and visceral drive that tend to dominate Solti's music. Still, in the crumbling Valhalla of Old Master conductors, the Hungarian maestro stands at the summit, along with a mere handful of survivors.

Solti aligns himself with the major conductorial forces of the day in that he, like Karajan and possibly one or two others, is at home in both opera and symphony, sharing the requisite talent, taste, and leadership. For him, it is important that he came out of an opera house, with the apprenticeship and coaching that both he and Karajan experienced in that milieu: "A whole other generation, from Toscanini to Kleiber to Furtwängler to Mahler, Strauss, and Walter, they all came on that ladder—people who came out of the theater as coaches. Then they had the balance of going back and forth, opera and symphony. This is missing." Solti offers his own career—the hard life, the battling for what he wanted, the waiting—as a model of the path the aspiring conductor should follow. At the same time, he also attributes much of what has happened to sheer good luck, to a knack for being in the right place at the right time. He admits, for instance, that had a proposed situation with the fledgling Chicago Lyric Opera come to pass, he would never have been invited to take over the Chicago Symphony, where he has enjoyed the greatest réclame of his career. At the time of the Lyric offer, he was newly ensconced as Generalmusikdirektor of the Frankfurt Opera, which eventually paved the way to his ten-year music directorship of the Royal Opera House at Covent Garden and then his move to Chicago, capping both aspects of his career.

The decade in London, Solti has said, made him a different person—more tolerant and broad-minded. "I was sort of a German pocket dictator. And I'm a little bit that—but fairer, more mellow." Part of this came from a driving ambition and a sense of being held back. He sees his early years as a "desperate situation," because after World War II he was already thirty-four and had not conducted anything. "That gave me the feeling that I will never catch up. I was trying to do everything as quickly as possible, as strong-mindedly as possible. There was that urge and not wanting to be obedient to anyone. But once you are safer

and well established and less ambitious, then you accept other points of view. Having been successful is a very great luxury."

George Solti was born in Budapest, where his first taste of opera came from his sister, a soprano, whom he accompanied in the standard arias. By age fourteen or fifteen he had already set his heart on becoming an opera conductor. At the time he was at the Liszt Academy seriously studying the piano as "a semi-child prodigy," a talented boy who played and who, since the family was poor, earned money by coaching singers and giving piano lessons. At eighteen Solti took a coaching job at the Budapest Opera. He spent the years 1932–39 in that house, and at twenty-four made his professional conducting debut with *Le Nozze di Figaro*. This traditional opera-house training offers tremendous advantages, "because you start with the most difficult material. Opera is much more difficult, much more complex material than symphony. If you begin to conduct opera, you surely have all the possibilities to conduct symphony, but never vice versa. Therefore it is much better to start and get a more all-around musical education as you work with singers. This is essential. I would not discard it for anything." Young Solti could have spent his years at home in Budapest, working his way up at the State Opera. But one of those early strokes of luck took him to the Salzburg Festival, where he appeared with a letter of recommendation from Budapest seeking permission for him to sit in on rehearsals. Asked if he could play some rehearsals, he began the very afternoon of his arrival with *Die Zauberflöte* under director Herbert Graf. When Toscanini stepped into the rehearsals, Solti stayed. That was 1936, and he returned the next summer as well, playing rehearsals for *Falstaff, Meistersinger, Fidelio*, the Verdi Requiem, and *Zauberflöte*—all the works under the Italian maestro. Moreover, he played the glockenspiel in the Mozart opera. Solti, naturally, fell under the spell of Toscanini, who for the decade 1936–46 became the Hungarian's musical ideal. But Solti also observed Knappertsbusch, Walter, and Furtwängler. Erich Kleiber, he claims, was a remarkable opera man who knew everything about the staging process and the look of opera.

Born a Jew, Solti stayed in Hungary until the last moment, August 1939, and then fled to Lucerne, where Toscanini had retreated with Adolf and Fritz Busch. Solti remained stuck there, playing the piano, until after the war. Although longing to go back to the Opera in Hungary, he learned that the Munich Opera needed a conductor at its new quarters in the Prinzregententheater. And so he went to the Bavarian city in 1946, leading *Fidelio* for the first time in his life. The Munich ensemble had stayed intact during the war, and Solti describes the situation as "an island" during the first few postwar years. He served as music director from 1946 to 1952, learning and conducting many works. Munich became a theater that played the *Ring* cycle, the Mozart repertory, and the major Strauss operas, and by the end of the Solti era it had seen some

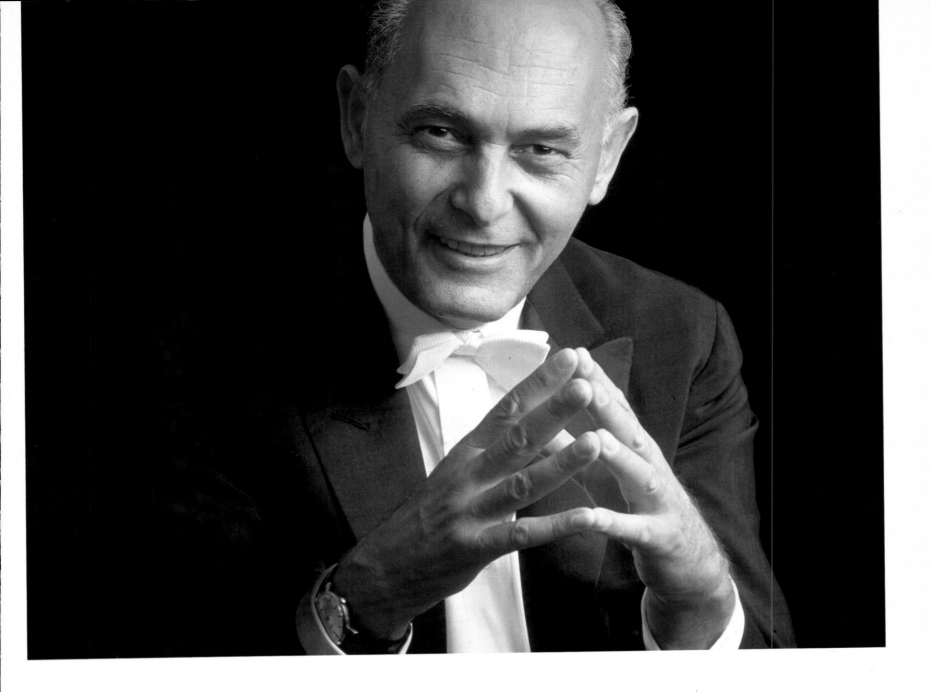

forty new productions. What Munich offered the maestro was an established musical style in the Mozart-Wagner-Strauss tradition handed down by Knappertsbusch and Krauss, together with an ensemble of such singers as Helena Braun, Maud Cunitz, Annelies Kupper, Hans Hotter, Franz Völker, Ferdinand Frantz, Lorenz Fehenberger, George Hann, and Hans Reinmar.

By 1953 Frankfurt had rebuilt its destroyed opera house, and Solti was asked to take over the music direction there. Drawing on his Munich apprenticeship, he set about organizing a new theater from scratch, and the ensemble of performers he put together included a number of the young Americans then flocking to Europe. In September 1953 Solti made his American debut with the San Francisco Opera, following this with performances in Chicago and then in 1960 at the Metropolitan. The year 1959 proved to be a turning point, since Solti had decided to abandon the opera house for an orchestral career. Meanwhile, an offer arrived from Covent Garden inviting him to become its music director in 1961, and when he consulted Bruno Walter, the advice was to accept. "This was basically the most enjoyable operatic time of my life," he has observed. Covent Garden had the orchestra, chorus, and technical foundation, and on this he proceeded to build. Among the things Solti is credited with in London is the emergence of the British singer at home

and on the international scene. But he brought quality to every aspect of Covent Garden's operatic activity. Then, in 1971, when he left London and took up the reigns of the Chicago Symphony, he was acting upon the decision he had made in 1959 to change the course of his development. Now he would concentrate on symphonic work. And the decision could be implemented because, thanks to his leadership of the historic *Ring* performances that Decca/London recorded in 1958–65 (with the Vienna Philharmonic and an all-star cast headed by Kirsten Flagstad, Birgit Nilsson, Régine Crespin, Christa Ludwig, Hans Hotter, James King, and Wolfgang Windgassen), Solti had gained interntional fame and respect of a sort seldom accorded to any conductor.

The key to such work and accomplishment, Solti believes, is the musical imagination. "That will distinguish you from another conductor. Only those people who have a clear and absolutely formed imagination are the ones you can rely on and who carry a performance. Without total imagination one is sunk. It is everything in music. I can't judge myself, but in my marrow bones I am really an opera conductor, a man of the theater." And as one listens to his music, there can be no doubt about it: George Solti is richly endowed with what the Germans call *Theaterblut.*

Leonard Bernstein

Great as his talent for music theater may be, Leonard Bernstein has allowed himself to be seduced into full, active involvement with opera only sporadically, but on each carefully chosen occasion, the episode has proved to be a notably important one, whether it was a matter of conducting Maria Callas at La Scala, of collaborating with Franco Zeffirelli at the Metropolitan Opera, or of creating a *Tristan und Isolde* project carried out simultaneously for radio, television, recording, and live performance. Aside from opera per se, most of Bernstein's career in music has had the theater at its core, just as his own compositions offer a programmatic blend of words, music, and even action. The large orchestral pieces are frequently text- or idea-inspired, and his collection of orchestral songs, *Songfest,* can be seen as studies for an opera. At one time Bernstein became the leading proselytizer for the belief that American musical theater would be the opera of the future, that musical comedy or Broadway musicals would fuse with opera. Some of what he foresaw has indeed come to pass, but the rest remains to be seen, for barriers still exist. From his earliest childhood in Massachusetts, Bernstein has always loved the voice, and his legendary collaboration with Russian mezzo Jennie Tourel began in the early 1940s. They gave joint recitals, and as he composed, she sang his songs and his symphonies.

But for all his fascination with opera, with musical theater, Bernstein has never plunged body and soul into that milieu. He prefers to come and go elusively, wherever the singers and the sense of drama engage him. La Scala beckoned for *Medea* and *La Sonnambula,* the Met for *Falstaff, Cavalleria Rusticana,* and *Carmen,* the Vienna State Opera for *Der Rosenkavalier, Falstaff,* and *Fidelio,* Munich for *Tristan.* In all Bernstein has led a little over a dozen operas in his entire career. Associates today say he probably would have done more had Callas continued her meteoric career, for it was her sizzling union of voice and theater that inspired—and at the same time spoiled—him in the mid-1950s. There has been nothing like her since, although today Bernstein is likely to proclaim that Hildegard Behrens is the closest thing in terms of intensity and intelligence. Behrens was his Isolde, and he tells how he wept when she came to his hotel room to sing the "Liebestod" for him before they embarked on Act III of *Tristan* in 1981.

At the soul of Bernstein and his work stands the exalted expression of the human voice—the fatalistic utterances of Mahler's songs, Beethoven's cry for freedom in *Fidelio,* the soaring lyricism of his own Broadway idiom, the patriarchal values of his own *Jeremiah* Symphony or *Mass* or Third Symphony. Bernstein is always listening to that inner voice. And this goes back to his twelfth year when he heard an aria over the radio sung by Jessica Dragonette. The drama of that voice riding the orchestral crest left a deep impression. He began to explore piano-vocal scores of *Aida, Carmen,* Gilbert and Sullivan, playing

On the Town and *Wonderful Town*, the former stretching the mold of the Broadway show in its use of music as a means of advancing the narrative. *West Side Story* (1957) took this idea even further and emerged as a kind of *durchkomponiert* musical. In 1952 Bernstein wrote his single opera to date, *Trouble in Tahiti*, but a sequel, commissioned by the Houston Grand Opera, is promised for 1983. *Candide*, in 1955, proved to be an intentional return to operetta, albeit a work of great sophistication in its wit and style. *Mass*, which Bernstein wrote for the opening of the John F. Kennedy Center for the Performing Arts in Washington in 1971, is a music-theater piece whose vast network of elements includes pop and religious music.

When it came to conducting opera, Bernstein began in 1946 with a student production at Tanglewood of the American premiere of Benjamin Britten's *Peter Grimes*, a work commissioned by Bernstein's mentor, Serge Koussevitzky. The maturing maestro's first professional stint in opera came on the highest rung of the ladder, at La Scala, and that happened unintentionally. He was in Italy for orchestral concerts, and Antonio Ghiringhelli pleaded with him to take over the opening of Cherubini's *Medea* at La Scala because music director Victor De Sabata was ill. Bernstein had not even heard of the work, but he looked at the score, fell in love with it, and accepted the Scala offer, despite feeling ill and exhausted from his own tour and having only ten days in which to prepare. Nor had he ever heard Maria Callas; indeed, he knew of her mainly as an alleged destroyer of conductors. After five days spent learning the music and selecting the cuts he felt necessary for the 1798 version of the score, he met with Callas for the first time and suggested cutting Medea's Act II aria for dramatic reasons. She understood him immediately. From that point on everything clicked, and the premiere became a tremendous triumph for all concerned. La Scala wanted him to return immediately. Finally the conductor accepted the new production of *La Sonnambula* scheduled for 1955, with Luchino Visconti directing, and he recalls the experience as "something marvelous, the closest to a perfect opera performance I've ever witnessed."

Scarcely begun, this skyrocketing opera career suddenly halted for awhile, as Broadway claimed Bernstein for *Candide* and *West Side Story*. Then in 1958 he accepted the directorship of the New York Philharmonic. But in 1964 he once again made room for opera, coming to the Met for *Falstaff*, which he later did in Vienna. In 1971, for the Beethoven Bicentennial, he led a new *Fidelio* at the Theater an der Wien, where the composer had first conducted the opera himself. In 1972 Bernstein was in the pit for opening night at the Met: a new opéra-comique version of *Carmen* with Marilyn Horne, a project now preserved on records. With the Philharmonic he devised a number of Wagnerian evenings: major scenes from *Tristan und Isolde*, sung by Jess Thomas and Eileen Farrell, and Act I of *Die Walküre* among them. All served as preparation for his Munich *Tristan* project, which stretched over months and months, each of the three acts conceived separately to ensure vocal freshness, intensity, and as deep a probing of the score as humanly possible. The maestro declares this to be the finest, most satisfying work he has done in what can only be characterized as a long and brilliant career. It is the expansiveness, the all-encompassing qualities of the theater—the richness and complexity of the form—that speak to Leonard Bernstein. But like so much that is paradoxical about his life and career, Bernstein's devotion to words and music, to theater, while undeniably genuine and profound, has been expressed in all too few trips to the opera house podium. Yet, each time he goes the distance, Leonard Bernstein makes history.

them at the piano and singing the tunes. Eventually, his sister Shirley joined him, becoming his first "diva." A passion for theater music was born. At fourteen Bernstein produced his first opera at the family summer home in Sharon, Massachusetts—a version of *Carmen* with rewritten libretto and lyrics, performed in the ballroom of a local hotel. Bernstein played the piano and sang, racing between his instrument and the stage. Later came *The Mikado*, *H.M.S. Pinafore*, and *The Pirates of Penzance*. At Harvard he produced and directed Marc Blitzstein's *The Cradle Will Rock* and played the piano for the performance. To Blitzstein he attributes enormous influence in the creation of musical theater with an American accent.

Despite this youthful mania, Bernstein's professional commitment to opera was long in coming, mainly because after substituting for the indisposed Bruno Walter in 1943, the young musician began his conducting career with the New York Philharmonic. In the meantime he also turned to Broadway with

Notes on the Photographs

When I began working as a portrait photographer, almost all my commissions came from artist managements. Today, it is usually the artists themselves who call, and one of the first questions they ask is: "What shall I wear?" And in the case of women: "What about makeup?" Concerning clothes, I have a standard answer: "As simple as possible." I like to focus on the face. Then, for a good session with maximum possibilities, I recommend that the sitter prepare both formal and informal clothes, and I usually ask for several changes with colors ranging from light to dark. The apparel required of men on stage is limited. Women, on the other hand, can dress in a great variety of ways, but for purposes of portrait photography, even they need to stay away from prints and vivid, complicated designs. As for makeup, it should be determined by whether the image is to be in color or black and white. With monochrome film, very little makeup may be necessary, but in color photography, a bit of paint and powder can frequently enliven an otherwise pale face. But making up for color must be done with great care, for retouching color is very expensive.

Many of my photographs are intended for use in publicity. That in itself suggests how the portrait should look. If it is to appear on flyers, on posters mounted before concert halls, or on record covers, the overall image must be attractive and interesting. The subject should seem to be dynamic and outgoing, and certainly as good-looking as nature and skill permit. Thus, the very demands of the situation generate tension, causing the sitter to fear our session may prove a failure. Many of the most eminent stars have arrived at my door declaring: "This is as bad as going to the dentist." No doubt the best portraits would be obtained if only the subject and I could spend a whole day together, even sharing a meal, the better to create an environment wherein the social encounter becomes the event, allowing the camera to be gradually forgotten. Since rapport is an essential element in the creation of a relaxed atmosphere, and a relaxed atmosphere constitutes a vital component of a productive photographic session, it is imperative that good rapport be established at an early moment. In meeting total strangers, I may find it impossible to like at first sight each and every person who arrives at my studio. But in order for me to take good pictures, I must come to like the subject, and whatever success I have in this regard can only increase my chances of being liked—an important factor in obtaining good responses from the sitter. Anything positive that I see in someone has to be examined, pointed out, and reinforced. Aided by this technique—one of my most valuable inventions—I end up liking virtually every one of my clients, however little we may seem to have in common at the outset.

After choosing the first garment to be worn, we go into the studio. It will have been set up in flat, overall lighting, which allows me to turn my subject to all sides without the time-consuming complications of shifting the lights constantly. Some people know what their most photogenic angle is; many, however, do not. It used to take me a while to find those angles. Now I can find them quickly; still, the first shots are made for that purpose. Once this has been done, we can proceed to a more inventive kind of lighting.

Most people have irregular features, with one eye smaller than the other, one cheekbone higher than its opposite, or a nose that points more to one side of the face. For the first, angle-seeking pictures, I work quite rapidly, and when my subject appears especially anxious about how he looks, I also try to do something that will divert his attention elsewhere. I might place the subject in an unorthodox position, or take the stage myself by telling a story designed to distract the sitter and draw him away from the concern over his looks.

For most of my photos made in the studio, I use strobe lighting. And I like the simplest lighting—usually one light, at the most two. Moreover, I still work with the same two Nikons and the same two Hasselblads that I purchased years ago.

Occasionally, we may move outside the studio and there work only by available light. The difference in approach is remarkable. In the studio I handhold the camera, for the speed of the strobe light permits me to try for the fleeting moment of expression, and once captured on film, the more fleeting that moment of expression, the more satisfying will the picture be for me. Outside the studio, where often the light is rather dim, I must stabilize the camera on a tripod and slow everything down—including the subject's movements—to accommodate the shutter speed. This means a less spontaneous picture, but sometimes one with a very special atmosphere, created by the diversity of natural light.

The sessions normally take at least three hours, which many people find excessive, but even so I have gone to four or five hours. It has always been my rule not to stop photographing until I think I have got the best. My concentration on the subject is total; thus, I feel drained when finally we finish and say: "Goodbye." After such an intense experience, the solitary activities of developing, printing, and often retouching are most welcome. These tasks may require an enormous amount of time, but they are all part of the creative process, and when carried out with patience and good music in the background, they can be very enjoyable.

Christian Steiner

Joan Sutherland

It was 2 P.M. on one of the hottest days in the summer of 1972 when my studio doorbell signaled the arrival of Joan Sutherland and Richard Bonynge for their photo session. Opening the door to greet them, I found a furious diva, a flustered conductor, and a foyer full of costumes, suitcases, and assorted paraphernalia. My doorman had failed me—probably due to heat prostration—and the famous couple had been forced to make several trips from their car to the elevator, carrying the baggage themselves. It took some airconditioned diplomacy to restore Sutherland's good spirits and Bonynge's equanimity, but the ensuing session went off without a hitch. It was very long, very relaxed, and, during our rest periods, Sutherland showed me candid pictures of their young son. When her husband left to keep an appointment, the soprano stayed on until well past 7 o'clock.

Elisabeth Schwarzkopf

Spring 1982. Schwarzkopf was in New York to launch her book about her late husband, Walter Legge, and I was to photograph her in a friend's elegantly appointed Park Avenue apartment. She arrived early, splendidly dressed in a blue evening gown (*ein blaues ding*, she called it) and accompanied by her friend Gustl Breuer. We began rearranging the precious furniture to the annoyance of an eccentric Chinese housekeeper, who refused to give the sleepy soprano a cup of coffee. Schwarzkopf took this with good humor, and we started to work. Then the master of the house arrived and suggested that we ought to take a portrait in front of the Dali painting in his dining room. Mercifully, the elderly gentleman was quite deaf and didn't hear the singer mutter under her breath: "I *hate* Dali!" Just as her patience was beginning to wear a bit thin I happened to mention that my father had been first violist of the Berlin Deutsche Oper when she sang her last Marschallin there in 1965. This brought the tired star to life as she spoke of my father, whom she knew quite well, and his four brothers, all musicians, with whom she had performed. The *gemütlich* session produced many charming photographs.

Placido Domingo

My files already contained several interesting shots of the Spanish tenor, all of them the products of a session held in 1976. For our 1982 encounter, however, I wanted him to pose in costume as Otello, one of his recent and greatest roles. It was rather difficult to arrange, given his busy schedule and the complicated maneuvering with the wardrobe department at the Met, where Maria Moore was of enormous help. Another member of the Met staff, Victor Callegari, spent two and a half hours doing Domingo's makeup. But the results made it all worthwhile. I took over one hundred pictures that afternoon. And with Domingo's extraordinary intelligence and natural sense of drama present in every one of them, the collection becomes a visual record of the art of operatic performance.

Maria Callas

I had always wanted to photograph Callas, but our appointments had always been canceled at the eleventh hour. Finally, in 1969, while I was in London recording a group of two-piano pieces with Earl Wilde, I received a call from John Coveney of Angel Records. He asked me to fly over to Paris and there shoot some pictures for a series that would encompass the highlights of the Callas repertory. Only a week earlier, the newspapers had been full of the Kennedy-Onassis marriage, and it occurred to me that the timing of the session was not the most propitious. Nevertheless, I called the Callas apartment upon my arrival in Paris, only to be politely informed that our appointment was postponed. The same conversation took place daily for one week. Even when I was standing in front of the door to her apartment on Rue Georges Mandel, I didn't believe the session would actually take place. But she appeared, in peignoir, hair flowing to the waist, gracious and charming. Callas had very definite opinions about how she should be photographed—opinions that didn't always coincide with mine. And I must confess that I chose to ignore some of her stronger assertions ("I must always be photographed from below or my nose looks too long!"). In the end, however, she seemed genuinely pleased with the results. Three years later, while in New York for the master classes she gave at the Juilliard, Callas came to my studio for a full-fledged photo session. Just before we finished, Giuseppe di Stefano joined us, and we all went out to dinner, during which this great lady apologized to me for all the postponements and cancellations I had endured in the past.

Jessye Norman

It was 1981. Daniel Barenboim was conducting Bruckner's *Te Deum* at Chicago's Symphony Hall, and I had photographed all but one of the principals for a Deutsche Grammophon recording. During the rehearsal I was overwhelmed by the sensual, velvet, enveloping voice of the soprano Jessye Norman. When the run-through was over, this wonderful singer announced in pear-shaped tones: "Now, I'm going to have my picture taken." She seated herself in front of a double bass and proceeded to chat with me amiably. A woman of amazing, monumental appearance, resembling a magnificent African sculpture, she moves with astonishing grace and dignity. The word for Jessye Norman is regal!

Victoria de los Angeles

As is my custom, I engaged de los Angeles in discussion to get her to relax and to inspire the widest gamut of facial expressions. I had previously photographed the Spanish soprano at her Hunter College recital with Alicia de Larrocha, and I told her how impressed I was with the fact that the pianist had played the entire program without music. De los Angeles did not share my enthusiasm. For a singer, she said, it can be quite unnerving not to be able to depend on the accompanist in a moment of lapsed memory.

Marilyn Horne

About thirteen years ago, I drove out to New Jersey to photograph Marilyn Horne in her home. Everything was set, and I took about six pictures when my Hasselblad broke down. Unfortunately, I was not prepared for this emergency and had to drive back to New York to fetch another camera. When I returned, embarrassed and slightly unnerved, we set to work again, only for the second camera to jam four pictures later. This time I took the offending monster apart and, somehow, got it back in working order. When the session was over, Horne gave me a record album inscribed: "I did not really break the camera." Three years later, in 1972, I was asked by Deutsche Grammophon to shoot a photo call at the Met rehearsal of Goeren Gentele's production of *Carmen*. Through some oversight, the singers had never been informed that I was coming, and everyone, including the makeup department, became quite upset. Remembering our previous encounter, Horne told me: "If it were anyone but you, I'd throw him out!" Sometimes, a little vicissitude goes a long way.

José Carreras

The only time we could arrange for a photo session was noon of the day Carreras had to fly back to Barcelona. His secretary asked that I send a car since the tenor's schedule was so tight. The request slipped my mind, and the morning of our appointment I frantically called limousine services until I found one that could comply. The man I spoke to was very laconic and off-hand, but when I asked what kind of car would be sent, he mustered a bit of indignation and assured me that his firm had only brand-new 1982 automobiles. I was somehow unconvinced, however, and taxied down to the meeting place, just to be sure. Standing in front of the hotel was a battered, old, red station wagon, its front caved in and its back full of garbage! I couldn't do anything about the front, but I did manage to clean up the rear of the jalopy, just in time to apologize when Carreras and his secretary appeared.
The singer was totally unconcerned about the state of his transportation and couldn't have been more gracious. When we got to my studio, Carreras was completely relaxed, posing proudly in his new brilliant-green jacket and stroking the beard he had just grown for his role as Rodolfo in the Zeffirelli production of *Bohème* at the Met. One moment the preening peacock and the next the introspective poet, Carreras revealed both lively intelligence and genuine sweetness in the resulting photographs.

Renata Tebaldi

The year was 1972, the city New York, and the subjects one of the greatest operatic teams of our time, Renata Tebaldi and Franco Corelli. Tebaldi wore her fabulous jewels—diamonds and sapphires—all glistening under the studio lights. A fan strategically placed in the background caused her veils to billow gently. The commanding presence of this great lady was awe-inspiring, and the session might have become too stiff and formal, had it not been for her little dog. Every time I unwrapped a packet of film, he stood up on his hindlegs in front of me, persuaded I was about to offer him something good to eat.

Leontyne Price

We met while standing on line at a movie theater. The discovery of mutual friends led to a dinner invitation to my house, where Price saw the pictures of Maria Callas I had just shot. She made an appointment then and there for a photo session several weeks later. The day before the session was to take place, we ran into each other at a concert, where she responded to my friendly greeting with a prima donna's hauteur. Anticipating that the sitting could be artificial and a headache, I decided to tease her about her "la-di-da" behavior when she turned up at my studio. With a very touching show of humility and insecurity, she apologized, saying that she still never knew quite how to act when she was "on display" in public. The session that followed was friendly and easy, just as the dinner party had been. Her earthiness and humor proved irrepressible. Gone was the distant diva, replaced by a warm and generous woman.

Sherrill Milnes

My first encounter with Milnes took place in 1977 when I photographed him in full makeup as Gilda's father for the London recording of *Rigoletto*, costarring Beverly Sills. When he came to my studio a year later for a portrait sitting, resplendent in a polka-dotted shirt, he appeared several decades younger. Tall, virile-looking, and endowed with enormous natural charm, the baritone dominates the studio as easily as he does the stage. Later that year, I was persuaded to come back from the country on Labor Day weekend to photograph Milnes and Sills for the cover of an album entitled *Up in Central Park*. An ornate, horse-drawn carriage provided transportation as the two stars, in their finery, sported about the park that fine day, causing quite a stir among the spectators.

Shirley Verrett

Sometimes, only the passage of time can provide the perspective necessary to evaluate the results of a photographic session. When I met with Verrett in 1971 for a very short sitting, I never succeeded in putting her at ease—in allowing her real personality to come through. She was accustomed to posing, as so many beautiful people are, and struck attitudes for the camera. The results were unsatisfactory to both of us. But years later, reviewing the pictures we had originally rejected, I found the portrait reproduced here quite lovely, revealing the artist to be outgoing, warm, and elegant.

Luciano Pavarotti

Pavarotti knows exactly how he wants to look and checks his poses constantly in any nearby mirror. He arrived at my studio announcing: "You must photograph me standing up. Clothes don't look well on me when I am sitting down." At that time, he weighed 330 pounds—"only thirty pounds overweight," he assured me. A man of strong opinions, the tenor always does his own makeup, unlike many artists. When we finished a rather difficult session in full costume as *Pagliacci* and Pavarotti was ready to leave, I was struck by the startling contrast in his appearance now that he was dressed in street clothes and sporting a fur hat with a yellow scarf wound round his neck. I persuaded him to return to the studio for a final series of pictures.

Renata Scotto

The first time I met Scotto it was for a portrait session in 1977. Although haughty and aloof, she graciously gave me all the time I needed, and I needed quite a bit. By talking to her nonstop and asking increasingly personal questions about her life and family, I got her to unbend, with the result that several of the shots came out very well. When we next worked together, some time later, she was modeling a chinchilla coat contributed to a Metropolitan Opera raffle. Standing in a box at the opera house, her hauteur is appropriate, her elegance fully apparent. Still later, in 1981, Scotto came to my new apartment, which she evidently found quite impressive, for her praise was extravagant. She had brought a huge bouquet of roses with which she wanted to pose. After three hours of makeup, the diva emerged, ready to be photographed. In contrast to our first session, she talked freely, mostly about her son, and the time flew by. When she left the roses went with her.

Mirella Freni

Without the complete cooperation of the Chicago Lyric Opera and its staff, my 1981 meeting with Mirella Freni could never have happened. They put me in touch with the soprano, who was singing in Texas, where, unfortunately, she had just broken her arm. They made the small theater available for our session, and allowed me to go through Freni's costumes for the forthcoming production of *Roméo et Juliette* so that I might choose something suitable for the sitting. All these details were finally worked out, and the session took place. I must say that Mirella Freni is as sweet and lovely in person as she appears to be on stage. Having been conditioned to expect famous artists to be pressed for time, I was nervous and tense as we began work, but my sitter reassured me that she had all afternoon and declared herself completely at my disposal. Here, for once, was a case of the subject reassuring the photographer, instead of vice versa. By carefully draping her costume, we even manged to disguise the cast on her arm. The session was a success and a delight.

Alfredo Kraus

When I first met Alfredo Kraus, he reminded me of an Italian matinee idol, dressed—à la Mastroianni—in impeccably tailored European clothes. We were scheduled to have two short sessions in Chicago, the first in the multicolumned foyer of the Opera House. He was soft-spoken, formal, and exceedingly polite during that rather public encounter. The next day, however, we were to work at his hotel. Meanwhile, the biggest snowstorm of the year struck Chicago, and not a taxi could be found, so I had to make my way, laden with all my equipment, through a foot and a half of snow. When I arrived soaking wet and exhausted, Kraus reacted with concern and personal warmth. His wife was present, watching us work as the tenor made up for his role in Gounod's *Roméo et Juliette*. He chatted away amiably, telling stories about the three generations of his family living under the same roof in Madrid. This was one time when the photographer's adversity provided the catalyst for establishing rapport with the subject.

Beverly Sills

Could there be *anyone* more spontaneous, effervescent, and charming than Beverly Sills, the darling of the opera stage and television screen? Given an audience, she exudes warmth, generosity, naturalness, and an irrepressible *joie de vivre*. You would never expect someone with her performing experience to freeze in front of a camera, but that is exactly what she does. I tried to ease her tension by asking questions and telling stories, but she always remained aware of the camera staring at her. Specific instructions, like "lean forward," "stretch your neck," and so on improved the situation, but did little to dispel the underlying constraint. Then John Coveney of Angel Records and Sills' good friend Tito Capobianco came in, and *voilà*, the consummate actress had the audience she needed! She sparkled with her accustomed vivacity; she leaned forward spontaneously; she arched her neck like a lovely swan! It's always easier to photograph Sills in costume. With her active intelligence and dramatic instinct, she assumes the character of the role, entering into it fully. At all times, however, her sense of humor is never far away, and our sessions were great fun—as well as hard work.

Frederica von Stade

From time to time, one encounters an opera star who seems curiously untouched by fame and success. Frederica von Stade (Flicka to her friends and countless admirers) is such a person. Well-bred, with an elegance that seems the natural by-product of a privileged childhood, she indulged in no displays of temperament during our long and enjoyable session. She took direction with the greatest ease, needing neither coaxing nor handling. Her husband, Peter Elkus, who is also a singer, was then learning the craft of photography and shadowed me— with my permission—throughout the session right into the darkroom.

Tatiana Troyanos

I arranged with Troyanos to select her clothes the day before our sitting. When I arrived at the singer's apartment as agreed, there was no answer to my ring. Yet I could hear the sound of singing inside, and so I continued pressing the doorbell—to no avail. Finally, fifteen minutes later, she opened the door, breathlessly apologizing for keeping me waiting. Troyanos is not the best-organized person I've ever met. Thus, to avoid problems, I gathered up the dresses we'd chosen for our session and placed them together in a corner of her closet. In this way she would have little difficulty remembering what our selections had been. The next day produced a blizzard. Would Troyanos show up? And with the clothes? I decided it would be safer to fetch her myself, and it was fortunate that I did, for she had quite forgotten what she was supposed to bring along. The session went wonderfully well. I had set the stage very carefully to create as theatrical an atmosphere as possible. In a candlelit room, she sat before a French brocade hanging, every inch the seductress. In another dramatic pose, she displayed a regal, dominating presence. Outside, the snow continued to fall.

Christa Ludwig

The doorbell rang, and there she stood—one of the greatest Marschallins of our time, wearing a simple print blouse, no makeup, sensible shoes! It was 1972, and I was to photograph Christa Ludwig for the cover of a Wagner album. Yet she had brought no costumes, no makeup expert, and no hairdresser—just herself. I was perplexed. What was I to do to transform this normal, unadorned lady into a glamorous figure from the magical world of operatic make-believe? The solution was minimal: I draped her upper torso in black velvet, placed her in front of a black ground, and allowed the penetrating intelligence behind that sensitive face to shine through. The result is, I think, a striking portrait. On sees a strong, assertive person who is unconcerned with trivialities and whose ego is secure enought to disappear. She expressed interest in what I was doing, asked perceptive questions, was totally at ease and self-contained. Glamour, it would seem, comes in many different guises.

Kiri Te Kanawa

Kiri Te Kanawa seems to thrive in the eye of the hurricane. I arrived for our session in an apartment overlooking Central Park where she had been staying in New York. Later in the day she was to return to London. Confusion and chaos reigned on all sides, yet the New Zealand soprano seemed totally unconcerned and completely relaxed. A secretary was typing letters in one corner of the living room, visitors came and went, the phone never stopped ringing. Te Kanawa was unperturbed. Once she was made up, the fun began. Lying on the floor, she put her legs up over the back of an armchair, arching her body so that her luxuriant hair streamed out on the carpet. "He'll have a photo session like he's never had before!" said she from her upside-down position. I went along with the joke, which, in the end, proved to be too much of a strain on her neck. Then we settled down for some serious picture-taking.

Gwyneth Jones

Both of the photo sessions I had with Gwyneth Jones were great fun. She is a beautiful, expansive person and every inch the diva. Besides, this lovely Welsh lady is completely fluent in German, and we rattled away in my mother tongue with great abandon. She has the rare ability to throw her head back and laugh, something that most people find very difficult to do. We got along famously, and after our first sitting, she invited me to the Met for her performance as the Marschallin in *Rosenkavalier*. Afterwards, she and her husband came to my home for a delightful, informal supper of cheese soufflé. The following year, Jones flew into New York just so I could photograph her as Helen of Troy in *Die ägyptische Helena*.

Janet Baker

Dame Janet is a lady. I've had occasion to observe her in public when she's been rather stiff, formal, and somewhat stuffy. But in the privacy of my studio, these qualities all disappeared, supplanted by naturalness, modesty, and genial candor. There was never the slightest sign of the diva beneath her unruffled composure, nor was there any anxiety about time during our session. In the portraits I tried to capture her intelligence and sympathetic warmth. As the session progressed, a girlish quality began to emerge, particularly in her unexpected, sunny smile.

Grace Bumbry

For our first photo session Bumbry arrived with her husband, both of them bubbling with enthusiasm about their new sportscar. Nothing would do but for me to take a spin around the park with her husband while Madame dressed. And so we sped away, racing around in circles, as I made appropriately enthusiastic noises. When finally I began shooting, Bumbry was rather stiff and formal, and I feared the pictures would turn out wooden and uninteresting. All this occurred early in my career, when I was constantly experimenting with ways to relax my subjects. Now I decided on something preposterous, and asked Bumbry to sit on the floor. Obviously, a *grande dame* doesn't sit on the floor, and this one was mildly outraged. But she complied, and, within minutes, the self-consciousness disappeared. Instead, a down-to-earth, rather lusty person emerged, transforming the session into a complete success. In our subsequent encounter, when I was to do some color shots for a forthcoming Carnegie Hall recital, Bumbry didn't wait to be asked: she sat right down on the floor, and we were off!

Nicolai Ghiaurov

At first the marvelous Bulgarian bass struck me as a big teddy bear. As soon as I arrived at his hotel in Chicago, late in 1981, he pulled out a book of production shots containing all the roles he had ever done. Then he brought out all his clothes so that we could pick something suitable for the sitting. A heavy accent sometimes made it a bit difficult to follow him, but the singer's sturdy sense of himself shone through. Ghiaurov is very good at taking direction. He also knew exactly which side of his face looked better, a rare thing among the subjects I have worked with. I could not leave before he had shown me his fur coats and sought my opinion of the fur hats he was considering. There was something endearing about him, something infinitely childlike.

Regina Resnik

I deeply regret that I have never had the opportunity to work closely with this dynamic artist. The photographs I made of her were taken for Columbia Record's album of Gian-Carlo Menotti's *The Medium*. Rather than in my studio, I shot during a photo call on stage at the Washington Opera in the 1968-69 season. Resnik's complete identification with her role—the mark of the consummate actress—somewhat obscures the witty, urbane lady underneath.

Jennie Tourel

I had photographed Jennie Tourel many times since our first session in 1967, always working in my studio. But this last portrait, made a year before she died, was done in her apartment on West 58th Street. Seated on an 18th-century *fauteuil*, Tourel wears pinned to her evening dress the order of the Legion d'Honneur, which a grateful France had conferred upon the singer for her contribution to French music. Surrounded by memorabilia and bibelots, she is every inch the *grande dame*. Could anyone ever guess that between poses she did the most hilarious and ribald imitations of every famous Carmen that ever trod the boards?

Birgit Nilsson

Everyone had told me about the Swedish soprano's legendary wit. But I'm afraid I never saw that side of her; at least I don't *think* so. She had warned me, when we made the appointment for our session, that she really didn't want to be photographed. She had a lot of shopping to do, and the session would have to be short. Thus prepared, I should have not been so surprised at the apparition that stood before my door at the appointed hour. Madame Nilsson had walked up Central Park West to my apartment as Aida in full regalia: costume, makeup, wig, and bangles. And New Yorkers think they have seen everything! The elevator man, admittedly, was in a state of shock. Despite the comic aspects of the situation, Madame Nilsson was brusque, businesslike, and impatient to get down to work. We spent forty-five intense minutes together, and she was gone—back down Central Park West, bangles blazing.

Nicolai Gedda

It is sometimes hard to tell whether the image one captures reflects the profoundest aspects of a personality or is merely a manifestation of a passing mood. With a person as complex as Gedda, it is almost impossible to make that distinction. I photographed him in 1972, and my initial impression was of a highly intelligent person with an acutely analytical mind. The tenor responded to direction easily, seeming to understand what I wanted before a sentence was half finished. Yet, as the session wore on, I became aware of a strong element of disdain that permeated his presence and flavored his conversation. My task became clear: to catch the moments when that negative aspect was not in evidence. Looking over the pictures, years later, I do believe that I had reasonable success. The person in the photograph strikes me as warm and friendly.

Herbert von Karajan

It was 1972, and Angel Records had asked me to photograph Karajan for several projects they were planning. I was aware of the conductor's reputation—both my brothers are in the Berlin Philharmonic—and I also knew that Karajan had a favorite photographer in Germany and didn't want to change. So it was with considerable fear and trembling that I approached my first meeting with the maestro. He let it be known that no sitting could last longer than 20 minutes, and that I had to be at his permanent disposition. The first day, the great man breezed in to conduct a *Fidelio* performance, *pünktlich* at 9 A.M. after an hour of jet-flying instruction, and I didn't see him until 3 P.M. *Genau* 20 minutes! And no conversation! This went on for days. His aides made suggestions of topics that, if broached, might help break through the barrier of icy coldness. For example, the astronauts had just come through Salzburg, and Karajan was fascinated by space travel. Now, however, the subject produced only a grunt. He turned up each day for our minisessions with his hair combed into an outrageous and unbecoming wave in front. Finally, I could bear it no longer, walked over to him, and mussed his hair. Sparks flew, but he said nothing, and eventually he got used to it. At one of our very last sessions, Madame von Karajan came in, and I was introduced by the maestro as "the brother of my Steiners." So he knew it all along! I realized that part of his technique in the perpetuation of the Karajan myth is to keep everyone around him off-balance and slightly insecure. I had no idea what he thought of the portraits, for I heard absolutely nothing for a good six months. Finally, I got word from Angel that he was in fact quite pleased, even insisting that Angel send me to Europe thereafter for all his record covers. Two years later I returned to photograph him again, and nothing had changed. He seemed not to recognize me, yet when we were ready to start shooting, he said: "Those were the best portraits I ever had. What shall we do next?" That was surely the longest sentence he ever addressed to me, and I began work in high spirits—while my subject immediately lapsed into total silence, as unapproachable as ever. I think the pictures reflect two basic aspects of the Karajan character: introspection and remoteness.

Erich Leinsdorf

I had met Erich Leinsdorf socially many times, yet it still came as a surprise when he called me himself, sometime in 1974, to make an appointment for a portrait sitting. It is well known that this highly organized man schedules himself to leave no moment wasted. But I had a second surprise when Leinsdorf arrived with a student in tow, laden with scores so the maestro could give him a conducting lesson while I worked with the camera! The student was more fortunate than I, for he received the larger portion of the sitter's attention. It was no mean feat to catch the stray moments when the lens and I were the objects of his undivided interest.

Karl Böhm

I spent fifteen minutes with the legendary German conductor in 1971—hardly enough to get a likeness, much less explore beyond the obvious. I regret this, for I had long admired this man whose career spanned so many generations of music-making. The occasion for our brief session was his endorsement of Acoustic Research Hi-Fi equipment, a sophisticated development he probably never could have envisioned when he began conducting early in this century.

James Levine

The only time I had ever photographed James Levine was for a performance at the piano with the Lasalle Quartet. But for a portrait of America's most protean opera figure, a full, formal session was in order. Miss Moody, his secretary, tried to arrange an appropriate time, and at least five appointments were made—and canceled. Levine's goodwill was never in doubt, but his commitments tend to be nonstop. Finally, I went to a rehearsal of the Verdi Requiem in early 1982 that was being held on the stage of the Met. Although his casual attire is not quite in keeping with the white-tie-and-tails image that projects from the pit, the exuberance and strength clearly evident in these action shots may be more representative of this exciting young conductor's musical personality.

Lorin Maazel

I flew to Cleveland to photograph Maazel for a recording of Prokofiev's *Romeo and Juliet*. We never got to exchange a word, but I tried to capture his intense concentration during a playback of the recording session. His is a strong, brooding face, and the pictures exude the strength and purposefulness of this young American conductor.

Claudio Abbado

My contact with Claudio Abbado has been purely social and, unfortunately, not very profound. I would like, some day, to photograph him in my studio, for this brilliant young conductor is a fascinating subject. He has an excellent profile and beautiful black hair that, in the photographs made in Chicago for a Deutsche Grammophon recording, was cut very short. His is a suave and controlled conducting style, characterized by the most elegant movements.

Georg Solti

It was September 13, 1971, and I had placed a call to Germany to wish my mother a happy birthday well in advance of my appointment with Sir Georg. Unfortunately, the call did not go through until the moment he crossed the threshold of my apartment. The maestro was accompanied by Hans Boon of London Records, for whom we were doing the session. I was about to cancel the call when Solti indicated that he was content to wait a bit. So, I spoke to Mother in German and paid my filial respects. Returning to my guests, I discovered that Solti had gleefully translated everything I had said for Boon's benefit and was in a benevolent and cheerful mood. (Boon later told me that Solti had been in foul humor when they arrived.) I was fascinated by Solti's appearance. The kinetic quality the great man displays on stage is belied by the sweetness of his facial expression, especially when he is talking animatedly. One therefore needs rapid reflexes to catch those moments of spontaneity and capture them on film. We worked very well together, and I was quite pleased with the resulting pictures.

Leonard Bernstein

Helen Coates, Bernstein's former piano teacher and subsequently his secretary, urged the maestro to have a sitting with me. Although reluctant, he finally agreed to spare all of forty-five minutes before a Philharmonic concert. It has always struck me as odd that the most exuberant and expansive performers are often fearful and withdrawn in front of the camera's scrutinizing eye. Bernstein most certainly was, and it took all my diplomacy and tact to get him to relax. Sensing that beneath the world-weariness was a kind and sympathetic man, I told him that I was suffering from enormous stage fright at the prospect of having so photogenic and famous a person pose for me. My little ploy worked, and the austere look disappeared from his face. He could not have been more solicitous and thoughtful in the brief moments we had together. Some time later, I was one of many photographers shooting a Boston Symphony television concert that he was conducting. Now I saw the public side of Bernstein in full panoply. His concentration and abandon—two seemingly contradictory traits—are very much in evidence in the picture reproduced here.